CLIMATE CHANGE ACT 2008 (UK)

Updated as of March 26, 2018

THE LAW LIBRARY

TABLE OF CONTENTS

Introductory Text

Climate Change Act 2008

2008 CHAPTER 27

An Act to set a target for the year 2050 for the reduction of targeted greenhouse gas emissions; to provide for a system of carbon budgeting; to establish a Committee on Climate Change; to confer powers to establish trading schemes for the purpose of limiting greenhouse gas emissions or encouraging activities that reduce such emissions or remove greenhouse gas from the atmosphere; to make provision about adaptation to climate change; to confer powers to make schemes for providing financial incentives to produce less domestic waste and to recycle more of what is produced; to make provision about the collection of household waste; to confer powers to make provision about charging for single use carrier bags; to amend the provisions of the Energy Act 2004 about renewable transport fuel obligations; to make provision about carbon emissions reduction targets; to make other provision about climate change; and for connected purposes. 9 [26th November 2008]

Be it enacted by the Queen's most Excellent Majesty, by and with the advice and consent of the Lords Spiritual and Temporal, and Commons, in this present Parliament assembled, and by the authority of the same, as follows:—

Part 1. Carbon target and budgeting

Part 1. Carbon target and budgeting

1. The target for 2050.

Net Zero Consideration means that it is now 100%

(1) It is the duty of the Secretary of State to ensure that the net UK carbon account for the year 2050 is at least 80% lower than the 1990 baseline.

(2) "The 1990 baseline" means the aggregate amount of—

    (a) net UK emissions of carbon dioxide for that year, and

    (b) net UK emissions of each of the other targeted greenhouse gases for the year that is the base year for that gas.

2. Amendment of 2050 target or baseline year

(1) The Secretary of State may by order—

    (a) amend the percentage specified in section 1. (1);

    (b) amend section 1 to provide for a different year to be the baseline year.

(2) The power in subsection (1)(a) may only be exercised—

    (a) if it appears to the Secretary of State that there have been significant developments in—

(i) scientific knowledge about climate change, or

(ii) European or international law or policy,

that make it appropriate to do so, or

(b) in connection with the making of—

(i) an order under section 24 (designation of further greenhouse gases as targeted greenhouse gases), or

(ii) regulations under section 30 (emissions from international aviation or international shipping).

(3) The developments in scientific knowledge referred to in subsection (2) are—

(a) in relation to the first exercise of the power in subsection (1)(a), developments since the passing of this Act;

(b) in relation to a subsequent exercise of that power, developments since the evidential basis for the previous exercise was established.

(4) The power in subsection (1)(b) may only be exercised if it appears to the Secretary of State that there have been significant developments in European or international law or policy that make it appropriate to do so.

(5) An order under subsection (1)(b) may make consequential amendments of other references in this Act to the baseline year.

(6) An order under this section is subject to affirmative resolution procedure.

3. Consultation on order amending 2050 target or baseline year

(1) Before laying before Parliament a draft of a statutory instrument containing an order under section 2 (order amending the 2050 target or the baseline year), the Secretary of State must—

(a) obtain, and take into account, the advice of the Committee on Climate Change, and

(b) take into account any representations made by the other national authorities.

(2) The Committee must, at the time it gives its advice to the Secretary of State, send a copy to the other national authorities.

(3) As soon as is reasonably practicable after giving its advice to the Secretary of State, the Committee must publish that advice in such manner as it considers appropriate.

(4) The Secretary of State may proceed to lay such a draft statutory instrument before Parliament without having received a national authority's representations if the authority does not provide them before the end of the period of three months beginning with the date the Committee's advice was sent to the authority.

(5) At the same time as laying such a draft statutory instrument before Parliament, the Secretary of State must publish a statement setting out whether and how the order takes account of any representations made by the other national authorities.

(6) If the order makes provision different from that recommended by the Committee, the Secretary of State must also publish a statement setting out the reasons for that decision.

(7) A statement under this section may be published in such manner as the Secretary of State thinks fit.

Carbon budgeting

4. Carbon budgets

(1) It is the duty of the Secretary of State—

(a) to set for each succeeding period of five years beginning with the period 2008-2012 ("budgetary periods") an amount for the net UK carbon account (the "carbon budget"), and

(b) to ensure that the net UK carbon account for a budgetary period does not exceed the carbon budget.

(2) The carbon budget for a budgetary period may be set at any time after this Part comes into force, and must be set—

(a) for the periods 2008-2012, 2013-2017 and 2018-2022, before 1st June 2009;

(b) for any later period, not later than 30th June in the 12th year before the beginning of the period in question.

5. Level of carbon budgets

(1) The carbon budget—

(a) for the budgetary period including the year 2020, must be such that the annual equivalent of the carbon budget for the period is at least [F134%] lower than the 1990 baseline;

(b) for the budgetary period including the year 2050, must be such that the annual equivalent of the carbon budget for the period is lower than the 1990 baseline by at least the percentage specified in section 1 (the target for 2050);

(c) for the budgetary period including any later year specified by order of the Secretary of State, must be such that the annual equivalent of the carbon budget for the period is—

(i) lower than the 1990 baseline by at least the percentage so specified, or

(ii) at least the minimum percentage so specified, and not more than the maximum percentage so specified, lower than the 1990 baseline.

(2) The "annual equivalent", in relation to the carbon budget for a period, means the amount of the carbon budget for the period divided by the number of years in the period.

(3) An order under this section is subject to affirmative resolution procedure.

F2. (4). . . . .

Amendments (Textual)

F1. Word in s. 5. (1)(a) substituted (31.5.2009) by Climate Change Act 2008 (2020 Target, Credit Limit and Definitions) Order 2009 (S.I. 2009/1258), arts. 1, 2. (2)

F2. S. 5. (4) omitted (31.5.2009) by virtue of Climate Change Act 2008 (2020 Target, Credit Limit and Definitions) Order 2009 (S.I. 2009/1258), arts. 1, 2. (3)

6. Amendment of target percentages

(1) The Secretary of State may by order amend—

(a) the percentage specified in section 5. (1)(a);

(b) any percentage specified under section 5. (1)(c).

(2) That power may only be exercised—

(a) if it appears to the Secretary of State that there have been significant developments in—

(i) scientific knowledge about climate change, or

(ii) European or international law or policy,

that make it appropriate to do so, or

(b) in connection with the making of—

(i) an order under section 24 (designation of further greenhouse gases as targeted greenhouse gases), or

(ii) regulations under section 30 (emissions from international aviation or international shipping).

(3) The developments in scientific knowledge referred to in subsection (2)(a) are—

(a) in relation to the first exercise of the power conferred by this section in relation to the percentage specified in section 5. (1)(a), developments since June 2000 (the date of the Royal Commission on Environmental Pollution's 22nd Report, "Energy – the Changing Climate");

(b) in relation to the first exercise of the power conferred by this section in relation to any percentage specified under section 5. (1)(c), developments since the evidential basis for the order setting that percentage was established;

(c) in relation to a subsequent exercise of any of those powers, developments since the evidential basis for the previous exercise was established.

(4) The power conferred by this section to amend the percentage in section 5. (1)(a) includes power to amend or repeal section 5. (4) (which directs that targeted greenhouse gases other than carbon dioxide are to be left out of account for the purposes of that provision).

(5) An order under this section is subject to affirmative resolution procedure.

7. Consultation on order setting or amending target percentages

(1) Before laying before Parliament a draft of a statutory instrument containing an order under section 5. (1)(c) (order setting target percentage) or section 6 (order amending target percentage), the Secretary of State must—

    (a) obtain, and take into account, the advice of the Committee on Climate Change, and

    (b) take into account any representations made by the other national authorities.

(2) The Committee must, at the time it gives its advice to the Secretary of State, send a copy to the other national authorities.

(3) As soon as is reasonably practicable after giving its advice to the Secretary of State, the Committee must publish that advice in such manner as it considers appropriate.

(4) The Secretary of State may proceed to lay such a draft statutory instrument before Parliament without having received a national authority's representations if the authority does not provide them before the end of the period of three months beginning with the date the Committee's advice was sent to the authority.

(5) At the same time as laying such a draft statutory instrument before Parliament, the Secretary of State must publish a statement setting out whether and how the order takes account of any representations made by the other national authorities.

(6) If the order makes provision different from that recommended by the Committee, the Secretary of State must also publish a statement setting out the reasons for that decision.

(7) A statement under this section may be published in such manner as the Secretary of State thinks fit.

8. Setting of carbon budgets for budgetary periods

(1) The Secretary of State must set the carbon budget for a budgetary period by order.

(2) The carbon budget for a period must be set with a view to meeting—

    (a) the target in section 1 (the target for 2050), and

    (b) the requirements of section 5 (requirements as to level of carbon budgets),

and complying with the European and international obligations of the United Kingdom.

(3) An order setting a carbon budget is subject to affirmative resolution procedure.

9. Consultation on carbon budgets

(1) Before laying before Parliament a draft of a statutory instrument containing an order under section 8 (order setting carbon budget), the Secretary of State must—

    (a) take into account the advice of the Committee on Climate Change under section 34 (advice in connection with carbon budgets), and

    (b) take into account any representations made by the other national authorities.

(2) The Secretary of State may proceed to lay such a draft statutory instrument before Parliament without having received a national authority's representations if the authority does not provide them before the end of the period of three months beginning with the date the Committee's advice was sent to the authority.

(3) At the same time as laying such a draft statutory instrument before Parliament, the Secretary of State must publish a statement setting out whether and how the order takes account of any representations made by the other national authorities.

(4) If the order sets the carbon budget at a different level from that recommended by the Committee, the Secretary of State must also publish a statement setting out the reasons for that decision.

(5) A statement under this section may be published in such manner as the Secretary of State thinks fit.

10. Matters to be taken into account in connection with carbon budgets

(1) The following matters must be taken into account—

(a) by the Secretary of State in coming to any decision under this Part relating to carbon budgets, and

(b) by the Committee on Climate Change in considering its advice in relation to any such decision.

(2) The matters to be taken into account are—

(a) scientific knowledge about climate change;

(b) technology relevant to climate change;

(c) economic circumstances, and in particular the likely impact of the decision on the economy and the competitiveness of particular sectors of the economy;

(d) fiscal circumstances, and in particular the likely impact of the decision on taxation, public spending and public borrowing;

(e) social circumstances, and in particular the likely impact of the decision on fuel poverty;

(f) energy policy, and in particular the likely impact of the decision on energy supplies and the carbon and energy intensity of the economy;

(g) differences in circumstances between England, Wales, Scotland and Northern Ireland;

(h) circumstances at European and international level;

(i) the estimated amount of reportable emissions from international aviation and international shipping for the budgetary period or periods in question.

(3) In subsection (2)(i) "the estimated amount of reportable emissions from international aviation and international shipping", in relation to a budgetary period, means the aggregate of the amounts relating to emissions of targeted greenhouse gases from international aviation and international shipping that the Secretary or State or (as the case may be) the Committee estimates the United Kingdom will be required to report for that period in accordance with international carbon reporting practice.

(4) Such amounts may be estimated using such reasonable method or methods as the Secretary of State or (as the case may be) the Committee considers appropriate.

(5) The duty in subsection (2)(i) applies if and to the extent that regulations under section 30 do not provide for emissions of targeted greenhouse gases from international aviation and international shipping in the budgetary period or periods in question to be treated as emissions from sources in the United Kingdom for the purposes of this Part.

(6) Section 30. (1) (emissions from international aviation and international shipping not to count as emissions from UK sources for the purposes of this Part, except as provided by regulations) does not prevent the Secretary of State or the Committee from taking into account the matter referred to in subsection (2)(i) for the purposes of this section.

(7) Nothing in this section is to be read as restricting the matters that the Secretary of State or the Committee may take into account.

Limit on use of carbon units

11. Limit on use of carbon units

(1) It is the duty of the Secretary of State to set a limit on the net amount of carbon units that may be credited to the net UK carbon account for each budgetary period.

(2) The "net amount of carbon units" means—

(a) the amount of carbon units credited to the net UK carbon account for the period in accordance with regulations under section 27, less

(b) the amount of carbon units debited from the net UK carbon account for the period in accordance with such regulations.

(3) The limit for a budgetary period must be set—

(a) for the period 2008-2012, not later than 1st June 2009, and

(b) for any later period, not later than 18 months before the beginning of the period in question.

(4) The Secretary of State must set a limit under this section by order.

(5) The order may provide that carbon units of a description specified in the order do not count towards the limit.

(6) An order under this section is subject to affirmative resolution procedure.

(7) Before laying before Parliament a draft of a statutory instrument containing an order under this section in relation to a budgetary period, the Secretary of State must—

(a) take into account the advice of the Committee on Climate Change under section 34. (1)(b) (advice on use of carbon units) in relation to that period, and

(b) consult the other national authorities.

Indicative annual ranges

12. Duty to provide indicative annual ranges for net UK carbon account

(1) As soon as is reasonably practicable after making an order setting the carbon budget for a budgetary period, the Secretary of State must lay before Parliament a report setting out an indicative annual range for the net UK carbon account for each year within the period.

(2) An "indicative annual range", in relation to a year, is a range within which the Secretary of State expects the amount of the net UK carbon account for the year to fall.

(3) Before laying a report under this section before Parliament, the Secretary of State must consult the other national authorities on the indicative annual ranges set out in the report.

(4) The Secretary of State must send a copy of the report to those authorities.

Proposals and policies for meeting carbon budgets

13. Duty to prepare proposals and policies for meeting carbon budgets

(1) The Secretary of State must prepare such proposals and policies as the Secretary of State considers will enable the carbon budgets that have been set under this Act to be met.

(2) The proposals and policies must be prepared with a view to meeting—

(a) the target in section 1 (the target for 2050), and

(b) any target set under section 5. (1)(c) (power to set targets for later years).

(3) The proposals and policies, taken as a whole, must be such as to contribute to sustainable development.

(4) In preparing the proposals and policies, the Secretary of State may take into account the

proposals and policies the Secretary of State considers may be prepared by other national authorities.

14. Duty to report on proposals and policies for meeting carbon budgets

(1) As soon as is reasonably practicable after making an order setting the carbon budget for a budgetary period, the Secretary of State must lay before Parliament a report setting out proposals and policies for meeting the carbon budgets for the current and future budgetary periods up to and including that period.
(2) The report must, in particular, set out—
    (a) the Secretary of State's current proposals and policies under section 13, and
    (b) the time-scales over which those proposals and policies are expected to take effect.
(3) The report must explain how the proposals and policies set out in the report affect different sectors of the economy.
(4) The report must outline the implications of the proposals and policies as regards the crediting of carbon units to the net UK carbon account for each budgetary period covered by the report.
(5) So far as the report relates to proposals and policies of the Scottish Ministers, the Welsh Ministers or a Northern Ireland department, it must be prepared in consultation with that authority.
(6) The Secretary of State must send a copy of the report to those authorities.

15. Duty to have regard to need for UK domestic action on climate change

(1) In exercising functions under this Part involving consideration of how to meet—
    (a) the target in section 1. (1) (the target for 2050), or
    (b) the carbon budget for any period,
the Secretary of State must have regard to the need for UK domestic action on climate change.
(2) "UK domestic action on climate change" means reductions in UK emissions of targeted greenhouse gases or increases in UK removals of such gases (or both).

Determination whether objectives met

16. Annual statement of UK emissions

(1) It is the duty of the Secretary of State to lay before Parliament in respect of each year, beginning with the year 2008, a statement containing the following information.
(2) In respect of each greenhouse gas (whether or not a targeted greenhouse gas), it must—
    (a) state the amount for the year of UK emissions, UK removals and net UK emissions of that gas,
    (b) identify the methods used to measure or calculate those amounts, and
    (c) state whether any of those amounts represents an increase or decrease compared to the equivalent amount for the previous year.
(3) It must state the aggregate amount for the year of UK emissions, UK removals and net UK emissions of all greenhouse gases.
(4) If in accordance with international carbon reporting practice a change of method is such as to require adjustment of an amount for an earlier year in the same budgetary period, it must specify the adjustment required and state the adjusted amount.
(5) If emissions of a greenhouse gas from international aviation or international shipping are not

required to be included in the statement by virtue of subsection (2), it must state any amounts relating to such emissions that the United Kingdom is required to report for the year in accordance with international carbon reporting practice.

(6) It must—

(a) state the total amount of carbon units that have been credited to or debited from the net UK carbon account for the year, and

(b) give details of the number and type of those carbon units.

(7) It must state the amount of the net UK carbon account for the year.

(8) It must state—

(a) the amount of net UK emissions of carbon dioxide for the year 1990,

(b) the amount of net UK emissions of each targeted greenhouse gas other than carbon dioxide for the year that is the base year for that gas, and

(c) a baseline amount for each greenhouse gas that is not a targeted greenhouse gas, determined on such basis as the Secretary of State considers appropriate.

(9) The amount referred to in subsection (8)(c) may be—

(a) the amount of net UK emissions of the gas for the year 1990 or a different year, or

(b) the average amount of net UK emissions of the gas for a number of years.

(10) The statement required by this section must be laid before Parliament not later than 31st March in the second year following that to which it relates.

(11) The Secretary of State must send a copy of the statement to the other national authorities.

17. Powers to carry amounts from one budgetary period to another

(1) The Secretary of State may decide to carry back part of the carbon budget for a budgetary period to the preceding budgetary period.

The carbon budget for the later period is reduced, and that for the earlier period increased, by the amount carried back.

(2) The amount carried back under subsection (1) must not exceed 1% of the carbon budget for the later period.

(3) The Secretary of State may decide to carry forward the whole or part of any amount by which the carbon budget for a budgetary period exceeds the net UK carbon account for the period.

The amount of the carbon budget for the next budgetary period is increased by the amount carried forward.

(4) Before deciding to carry an amount back or forward under this section, the Secretary of State must—

(a) consult the other national authorities, and

(b) obtain, and take into account, the advice of the Committee on Climate Change.

(5) Any such decision must be made no later than 31st May in the second year after the end of the earlier of the two budgetary periods affected.

18. Final statement for budgetary period

(1) It is the duty of the Secretary of State to lay before Parliament in respect of each budgetary period a statement containing the following information.

(2) In respect of each targeted greenhouse gas, it must state the final amount for the period of UK emissions, UK removals and net UK emissions of that gas.

That is the total of the amounts (or adjusted amounts) stated under section 16 (annual statement of UK emissions) in respect of that gas for the years included in the period.

(3) It must—

(a) state the final amount of carbon units that have been credited to or debited from the net UK carbon account for the period, and

(b) give details of the number and type of those carbon units.

(4) It must state the final amount of the net UK carbon account for the period.

(5) It must state whether the Secretary of State has decided to carry an amount back under section 17. (1) (power to carry amount back from the budget for the next budgetary period), and if so what amount.

(6) It must state the amount of the carbon budget for the period.

That is the amount originally set, subject to any exercise of the powers conferred by section 17 (powers to carry amounts from one budgetary period to another) and any alteration of the budget under section 21.

(7) Whether the carbon budget for a period has been met shall be determined by reference to the figures given in the statement laid before Parliament under this section in respect of that period.

(8) If the carbon budget for the period has not been met, the statement must explain why it has not been met.

(9) The statement required by this section must be laid before Parliament not later than 31st May in the second year following the end of the period to which it relates.

(10) The Secretary of State must send a copy of the statement to the other national authorities.

19. Duty to report on proposals and policies for compensating for budget excess

(1) As soon as is reasonably practicable after laying a statement before Parliament under section 18 in respect of a period for which the net UK carbon account exceeds the carbon budget, the Secretary of State must lay before Parliament a report setting out proposals and policies to compensate in future periods for the excess emissions.

(2) So far as the report relates to proposals and policies of the Scottish Ministers, the Welsh Ministers or a Northern Ireland department, it must be prepared in consultation with that authority.

(3) The Secretary of State must send a copy of the report to those authorities.

20. Final statement for 2050.

(1) It is the duty of the Secretary of State to lay before Parliament in respect of the year 2050 a statement containing the following information.

(2) In respect of each targeted greenhouse gas, it must state the amount for that year of UK emissions, UK removals and net UK emissions of that gas.

That is the amount stated for that year in respect of that gas under section 16 (annual statement of UK emissions).

(3) It must—

(a) state the amount of carbon units that have been credited to or debited from the net UK carbon account for the year, and

(b) give details of the number and type of those carbon units.

(4) It must state the amount of the net UK carbon account for that year.

(5) Whether the target in section 1 (the target for 2050) has been met shall be determined by reference to the figures given in the statement laid before Parliament under this section.

(6) If the target has not been met, the statement must explain why it has not been met.

(7) The statement required by this section must be laid before Parliament not later than 31st May 2052.

(8) The Secretary of State must send a copy of the statement to the other national authorities.

Alteration of budgets or budgetary periods

21. Alteration of carbon budgets

(1) An order setting the carbon budget for a period may not be revoked after the date by which a budget for the period was required to be set.

(2) An order setting the carbon budget for a period may be amended after the date by which a budget for the period was required to be set only if it appears to the Secretary of State that, since the budget was originally set (or previously altered), there have been significant changes affecting the basis on which the previous decision was made.

(3) An order setting the carbon budget for a period may be amended after the period has begun only if it appears to the Secretary of State that there have been such changes since the period began.

(4) An order setting the carbon budget for a period may not be amended after the period has ended.

(5) An order revoking or amending an order setting a carbon budget is subject to affirmative resolution procedure.

22. Consultation on alteration of carbon budgets

(1) Before laying before Parliament a draft of a statutory instrument containing an order under section 21 (alteration of carbon budgets), the Secretary of State must—

    (a) obtain, and take into account, the advice of the Committee on Climate Change, and

    (b) take into account any representations made by the other national authorities.

(2) The Committee must, at the time it gives its advice to the Secretary of State, send a copy to the other national authorities.

(3) As soon as is reasonably practicable after giving its advice to the Secretary of State, the Committee must publish that advice in such manner as it considers appropriate.

(4) The Secretary of State may proceed to lay such a draft statutory instrument before Parliament without having received a national authority's representations if the authority does not provide them before the end of the relevant period.

(5) The relevant period is—

    (a) if the budgetary period to which the order relates has begun, one month beginning with the date the Committee's advice was sent to the authority, or

    (b) otherwise, three months beginning with that date.

(6) At the same time as laying such a draft statutory instrument before Parliament, the Secretary of State must publish a statement setting out whether and how the order takes account of any representations made by the other national authorities.

(7) If the order makes provision different from that recommended by the Committee, the Secretary of State must also publish a statement setting out the reasons for that decision.

(8) A statement under this section may be published in such manner as the Secretary of State thinks fit.

23. Alteration of budgetary periods

(1) The Secretary of State may by order amend section 4. (1)(a) so as to alter—

    (a) the length of the budgetary periods, or

    (b) the dates in the calendar year on which the budgetary periods begin and end.

(2) This power may only be exercised if it appears to the Secretary of State necessary to do so in order to keep the budgetary periods under this Part in line with similar periods under any agreement at European or international level to which the United Kingdom is a party.

(3) The power may not be exercised in such a way that any period falls outside a budgetary period.

(4) An order may make such consequential amendments of the provisions of this Act as appear to the Secretary of State to be necessary or expedient.

(5) Before making an order under this section the Secretary of State must consult the other national authorities.

(6) An order under this section is subject to affirmative resolution procedure.

Modifications etc. (not altering text)

C1. S. 23. (4) power to amend conferred (18.12.2013) by Energy Act 2013 (c. 32), ss. 1. (8)(a), 156. (3)

Targeted greenhouse gases

24. Targeted greenhouse gases

(1) In this Part a "targeted greenhouse gas" means—
   (a) carbon dioxide,
   (b) methane,
   (c) nitrous oxide,
   (d) hydrofluorocarbons,
   (e) perfluorocarbons,
   (f) sulphur hexafluoride, and
   (g) any other greenhouse gas designated as a targeted greenhouse gas by order made by the Secretary of State.

(2) The order may make such consequential amendments of the provisions of this Act as appear to the Secretary of State to be necessary or expedient.

(3) Before making an order under this section, the Secretary of State must—
   (a) consult the other national authorities, and
   (b) obtain, and take into account, the advice of the Committee on Climate Change.

(4) As soon as is reasonably practicable after giving its advice to the Secretary of State, the Committee must publish that advice in such manner as it considers appropriate.

(5) If the order makes provision different from that recommended by the Committee, the Secretary of State must publish a statement setting out the reasons for that decision.

(6) The statement may be published in such manner as the Secretary of State thinks fit.

(7) An order under this section is subject to affirmative resolution procedure.

25. Base years for targeted greenhouse gases other than CO2.

(1) The base years for the purposes of this Act for targeted greenhouse gases other than carbon dioxide are—

Gas	Base year
methane	1990
nitrous oxide	1990
hydrofluorocarbons	1995
perfluorocarbons	1995
sulphur hexafluoride	1995

(2) The Secretary of State may make provision by order amending the table in subsection (1) so as to—
   (a) specify the base year for a gas designated as a targeted greenhouse gas by order under section 24. (1), or
   (b) specify a different base year from that for the time being specified in relation to any targeted greenhouse gas other than carbon dioxide.

(3) An order may—

(a) designate a particular base year, or

(b) designate a number of base years and provide that the average amount of net UK emissions of a gas for those years is to be treated for the purposes of this Act as the amount of net UK emissions for the base year.

(4) The power in subsection (2)(b) may only be exercised if it appears to the Secretary of State that there have been significant developments in European or international law or policy that make it appropriate to do so.

(5) Before making an order under this section, the Secretary of State must—

(a) consult the other national authorities, and

(b) obtain, and take into account, the advice of the Committee on Climate Change.

(6) As soon as is reasonably practicable after giving its advice to the Secretary of State, the Committee must publish that advice in such manner as it considers appropriate.

(7) If the order makes provision different from that recommended by the Committee, the Secretary of State must publish a statement setting out the reasons for that decision.

(8) The statement may be published in such manner as the Secretary of State thinks fit.

(9) An order under this section is subject to affirmative resolution procedure.

Carbon units, carbon accounting and the net UK carbon account

26. Carbon units and carbon accounting

(1) In this Part a "carbon unit" means a unit of a kind specified in regulations made by the Secretary of State and representing—

(a) a reduction in an amount of greenhouse gas emissions,

(b) the removal of an amount of greenhouse gas from the atmosphere, or

(c) an amount of greenhouse gas emissions allowed under a scheme or arrangement imposing a limit on such emissions.

(2) The Secretary of State may make provision by regulations for a scheme—

(a) for registering or otherwise keeping track of carbon units, or

(b) for establishing and maintaining accounts in which carbon units may be held, and between which they may be transferred, by the Secretary of State.

The regulations may, in particular, provide for an existing scheme to be adapted for these purposes.

(3) The regulations may make provision—

(a) appointing a body to administer the scheme;

(b) establishing a body for that purpose and making such provision in relation to the appointment of members, staffing, expenditure, procedure and otherwise as the Secretary of State considers appropriate;

(c) conferring power on the Secretary of State to give guidance or directions to the body administering the scheme;

(d) conferring power on the Secretary of State to delegate the performance of any of the functions conferred or imposed on the Secretary of State by the regulations;

(e) requiring the payment by persons using the scheme of charges (of an amount determined by or under the regulations) towards the cost of operating it.

(4) If an existing body is appointed to administer the scheme, the regulations may make such modifications of any enactment relating to that body as the Secretary of State considers appropriate.

27. Net UK carbon account

(1) In this Part the "net UK carbon account" for a period means the amount of net UK emissions of targeted greenhouse gases for the period—

(a) reduced by the amount of carbon units credited to the net UK carbon account for the period in accordance with regulations under this section, and

(b) increased by the amount of carbon units that in accordance with such regulations are to be debited from the net UK carbon account for the period.

(2) The net amount of carbon units credited to the net UK carbon account for a budgetary period must not exceed the limit set under section 11 (limit on use of carbon units) for the period.

(3) The Secretary of State must make provision by regulations about—

(a) the circumstances in which carbon units may be credited to the net UK carbon account for a period,

(b) the circumstances in which such units must be debited from that account for a period, and

(c) the manner in which this is to be done.

(4) The regulations must contain provision for ensuring that carbon units that are credited to the net UK carbon account for a period cease to be available to offset other greenhouse gas emissions.

(5) The regulations must contain provision—

(a) for determining whether the total amount of carbon units allocated to the United Kingdom for each budgetary period under schemes or arrangements imposing a limit on emissions from sources in the United Kingdom represent an amount of net UK emissions of targeted greenhouse gases for the period greater than the carbon budget for the period, and

(b) for ensuring that, if this is the case, carbon units representing the amount of such emissions in excess of the budget are not used to offset greenhouse gas emissions in the United Kingdom or elsewhere.

28. Procedure for regulations under section 26 or 27.

(1) The following provisions apply in relation to regulations under section 26 (carbon units and carbon accounting) or section 27 (net UK carbon account).

(2) The regulations are subject to affirmative resolution procedure if—

(a) they are the first regulations to be made under those sections,

(b) they specify a carbon unit of a kind not previously specified in regulations made under those sections,

(c) they alter the amount by which—

(i) a carbon unit that is credited to the net UK carbon account for a period reduces the net UK carbon account for that period, or

(ii) a carbon unit that is debited from the net UK carbon account for a period increases the net UK carbon account for that period, or

(d) they make modifications of an enactment contained in primary legislation.

(3) Otherwise the regulations are subject to negative resolution procedure.

(4) The Secretary of State must consult the other national authorities—

(a) in the case of regulations subject to affirmative resolution procedure, before laying before Parliament a draft of a statutory instrument containing the regulations;

(b) in the case of regulations subject to negative resolution procedure, before making the regulations.

(5) The Secretary of State must obtain, and take into account, the advice of the Committee on Climate Change before laying before Parliament a draft of a statutory instrument containing—

(a) the first regulations to be made under those sections, or

(b) regulations making provision of the kind described in paragraph (b) or (c) of subsection (2).

Other supplementary provisions

29. UK emissions and removals of greenhouse gases

(1) In this Part—

(a) "UK emissions", in relation to a greenhouse gas, means emissions of that gas from sources in the United Kingdom;

(b) "UK removals", in relation to a greenhouse gas, means removals of that gas from the atmosphere due to land use, land-use change or forestry activities in the United Kingdom;

(c) the "net UK emissions" for a period, in relation to a greenhouse gas, means the amount of UK emissions of that gas for the period reduced by the amount for the period of UK removals of that gas.

(2) The amount of UK emissions and UK removals of a greenhouse gas for a period must be determined consistently with international carbon reporting practice.

30. Emissions from international aviation or international shipping

(1) Emissions of greenhouse gases from international aviation or international shipping do not count as emissions from sources in the United Kingdom for the purposes of this Part, except as provided by regulations made by the Secretary of State.

(2) The Secretary of State may by order define what is to be regarded for this purpose as international aviation or international shipping.

Any such order is subject to affirmative resolution procedure.

(3) The Secretary of State must, before expiry of the period ending with 31st December 2012—

(a) make provision by regulations as to the circumstances in which, and the extent to which, emissions from international aviation or international shipping are to be regarded for the purposes of this Part as emissions from sources in the United Kingdom, or

(b) lay before Parliament a report explaining why regulations making such provision have not been made.

(4) The expiry of the period mentioned in subsection (3) does not affect the power of the Secretary of State to make regulations under this section.

(5) Regulations under this section—

(a) may make provision only in relation to emissions of a targeted greenhouse gas;

(b) may, in particular, provide for such emissions to be regarded as emissions from sources in the United Kingdom if they relate to the transport of passengers or goods to or from the United Kingdom.

(6) Regulations under this section may make provision—

(a) as to the period or periods (whether past or future) in which emissions of the targeted greenhouse gas are to be taken into account as UK emissions of that gas, and

(b) as to the manner in which such emissions are to be taken into account in determining UK emissions of that gas for the year that is the base year for that gas.

(7) They may, in particular—

(a) designate a different base year, or

(b) designate a number of base years,

and provide for the emissions in that year, or the average amount of emissions in those years, to be treated for the purposes of this Act as UK emissions of that gas for the year that is the base year for that gas.

(8) For the purposes of this section the base year for carbon dioxide is the year that is the baseline year for the purposes of this Part.

31. Procedure for regulations under section 30.

(1) Before making regulations under section 30, the Secretary of State must obtain, and take into account, the advice of the Committee on Climate Change.

(2) As soon as is reasonably practicable after giving its advice to the Secretary of State, the Committee must publish that advice in such manner as it considers appropriate.

(3) If the regulations make provision different from that recommended by the Committee, the Secretary of State must publish a statement setting out the reasons for that decision.

(4) The statement may be published in such manner as the Secretary of State thinks fit.

(5) Regulations under section 30 are subject to affirmative resolution procedure.

Part 2. The Committee on Climate Change

Part 2. The Committee on Climate Change

32. The Committee on Climate Change

(1) There shall be a body corporate to be known as the Committee on Climate Change or, in Welsh, as y Pwyllgor ar Newid Hinsawdd (referred to in this Part as "the Committee").

(2) Schedule 1 contains further provisions about the Committee.

Functions of the Committee

33. Advice on level of 2050 target

(1) It is the duty of the Committee to advise the Secretary of State on—

    (a) whether the percentage specified in section 1. (1) (the target for 2050) should be amended, and

    (b) if so, what the amended percentage should be.

(2) Advice given by the Committee under this section must also contain the reasons for that advice.

(3) The Committee must give its advice under this section not later than 1st December 2008.

(4) The Committee must, at the time it gives its advice under this section to the Secretary of State, send a copy to the other national authorities.

(5) As soon as is reasonably practicable after giving its advice to the Secretary of State, the Committee must publish that advice in such manner as it considers appropriate.

34. Advice in connection with carbon budgets

(1) It is the duty of the Committee to advise the Secretary of State, in relation to each budgetary period, on—

    (a) the level of the carbon budget for the period,

    (b) the extent to which the carbon budget for the period should be met—

(i) by reducing the amount of net UK emissions of targeted greenhouse gases, or

(ii) by the use of carbon units that in accordance with regulations under sections 26 and 27 may be credited to the net UK carbon account for the period,

    (c) the respective contributions towards meeting the carbon budget for the period that should be made—

(i) by the sectors of the economy covered by trading schemes (taken as a whole);

(ii) by the sectors of the economy not so covered (taken as a whole), and

(d) the sectors of the economy in which there are particular opportunities for contributions to be made towards meeting the carbon budget for the period through reductions in emissions of targeted greenhouse gases.

(2) In relation to the budgetary period 2008-2012, the Committee must also advise the Secretary of State on—

(a) whether it would be consistent with its advice on the level of the carbon budget for the period to set a carbon budget such that the annual equivalent for the period was lower than the 1990 baseline by 20%, and

(b) the costs and benefits of setting such a budget.

(3) Advice given by the Committee under this section must also contain the reasons for that advice.

(4) The Committee must give its advice under this section—

(a) for the budgetary periods 2008-2012, 2013-2017 and 2018-2022, not later than 1st December 2008;

(b) for any later period, not later than six months before the last date for setting the carbon budget for the period (see section 4. (2)(b)).

(5) The Committee must, at the time it gives its advice under this section to the Secretary of State, send a copy to the other national authorities.

(6) As soon as is reasonably practicable after giving its advice under this section the Committee must publish that advice in such manner as it considers appropriate.

35. Advice on emissions from international aviation and international shipping

(1) It is the duty of the Committee to advise the Secretary of State on the consequences of treating emissions of targeted greenhouse gases from—

(a) international aviation, and

(b) international shipping,

as emissions from sources in the United Kingdom for the purposes of Part 1.

(2) The duty applies if and to the extent that regulations under section 30 do not provide for such emissions to be so treated.

(3) Advice given by the Committee under this section must also contain the reasons for that advice.

(4) The Committee must give its advice under this section—

(a) when it gives its advice under section 34 for the budgetary period 2023-2027, and

(b) when it gives its advice under that section for each subsequent budgetary period.

(5) The Committee must, at the time it gives its advice under this section to the Secretary of State, send a copy to the other national authorities.

(6) As soon as is reasonably practicable after giving its advice to the Secretary of State, the Committee must publish that advice in such manner as it considers appropriate.

36. Reports on progress

(1) It is the duty of the Committee to lay before Parliament and each of the devolved legislatures each year, beginning with the year 2009, a report setting out the Committee's views on—

(a) the progress that has been made towards meeting the carbon budgets that have been set under Part 1 and the target in section 1 (the target for 2050),

(b) the further progress that is needed to meet those budgets and that target, and

(c) whether those budgets and that target are likely to be met.

(2) The Committee's report in the second year after the end of a budgetary period must also set out the Committee's general views on—

(a) the way in which the budget for the period was or was not met, and

(b) action taken during the period to reduce net UK emissions of targeted greenhouse gases.

(3) The first report under this section must be laid before Parliament and the devolved legislatures not later than 30th September 2009.

(4) Each subsequent report under this section, other than one in the second year after the end of a budgetary period, must be laid before Parliament and the devolved legislatures not later than 30th June in the year in which it is made.

(5) A report in the second year after the end of a budgetary period must be laid before Parliament and the devolved legislatures not later than 15th July in the year in which it is made.

(6) The Secretary of State may by order extend the period mentioned in subsection (4) or (5).

(7) Before making such an order the Secretary of State must consult the other national authorities.

(8) Any such order is subject to negative resolution procedure.

37. Response to Committee's reports on progress

(1) The Secretary of State must lay before Parliament a response to the points raised by each report of the Committee under section 36 (reports on progress).

(2) Before doing so, the Secretary of State must consult the other national authorities on a draft of the response.

(3) The response to the Committee's first report under section 36 must be laid before Parliament not later than 15th January 2010.

(4) Each subsequent response must be laid before Parliament not later than 15th October in the year in which the Committee's report is made.

(5) The Secretary of State may by order extend that period.

(6) Any such order is subject to negative resolution procedure.

38. Duty to provide advice or other assistance on request

(1) The Committee must, at the request of a national authority, provide advice, analysis, information or other assistance to the authority in connection with—

(a) the authority's functions under this Act,

(b) the progress made towards meeting the objectives set by or under this Act,

(c) adaptation to climate change, or

(d) any other matter relating to climate change.

(2) In particular, the Committee must, at the request of a national authority—

(a) advise the authority about any limit proposed to be set by a trading scheme on the total amount of the activities to which the scheme applies, or

(b) assist the authority in connection with the preparation of statistics relating to greenhouse gas emissions.

(3) The Committee must, at the request of a national authority other than the Secretary of State, provide advice, analysis, information or other assistance to the authority in connection with any target, budget or similar requirement relating to emissions of greenhouse gas that has been adopted by the authority or to which the authority is otherwise subject.

Supplementary provisions

39. General ancillary powers

(1) The Committee may do anything that appears to it necessary or appropriate for the purpose of, or in connection with, the carrying out of its functions.

(2) In particular the Committee may—

    (a) enter into contracts,

    (b) acquire, hold and dispose of property,

    (c) borrow money,

    (d) accept gifts, and

    (e) invest money.

(3) In exercising its functions, the Committee may—

    (a) gather information and carry out research and analysis,

    (b) commission others to carry out such activities, and

    (c) publish the results of such activities carried out by the Committee or others.

(4) The Committee must have regard to the desirability of involving the public in the exercise of its functions.

40. Grants to the Committee

A national authority may make grants to the Committee of such amount and subject to such conditions as the authority thinks fit.

41. Powers to give guidance

(1) The national authorities may give the Committee guidance as to the matters it is to take into account in the exercise of—

    (a) its functions generally, or

    (b) any of its functions under Schedule 1.

(2) The Secretary of State may give the Committee guidance as to the matters it is to take into account in the exercise of its functions under—

    (a) Part 1 (carbon target and budgeting),

    (b) section 33 (advice on level of 2050 target),

    (c) section 34 (advice in connection with carbon budgets),

    (d) section 35 (advice on emissions from international aviation and international shipping),

    (e) section 36 (reports on progress),

    (f) section 57 (advice on report on impact of climate change), or

    (g) section 59 (reporting on progress in connection with adaptation).

Before giving guidance under any of paragraphs (a) to (f), the Secretary of State must consult the other national authorities.

(3) A national authority that requests the Committee to provide advice, analysis, information or other assistance under—

    (a) section 38 (duty to provide advice or assistance on request), or

    (b) section 48 (advice on trading scheme regulations),

may give the Committee guidance as to the matters it is to take into account in responding to that request.

If the request is made by two or more national authorities, the guidance must be given by them jointly.

(4) The power to give guidance under this section includes power to vary or revoke it.

(5) In performing its functions the Committee must have regard to any guidance given under this section.

42. Powers to give directions

(1) The national authorities may give the Committee directions as to the exercise of—

    (a) its functions generally, or

    (b) any of its functions under Schedule 1.

(2) The Secretary of State may give the Committee directions as to the exercise of its functions under—

    (a) Part 1 (carbon target and budgeting),

    (b) section 33 (advice on level of 2050 target),

    (c) section 34 (advice in connection with carbon budgets),

    (d) section 35 (advice on emissions from international aviation and international shipping),

    (e) section 36 (reports on progress),

    (f) section 57 (advice on report on impact of climate change), or

    (g) section 59 (reporting on progress in connection with adaptation).

Before giving directions under any of paragraphs (a) to (f), the Secretary of State must consult the other national authorities.

(3) A national authority that requests the Committee to provide advice, analysis, information or other assistance under—

    (a) section 38 (duty to provide advice or assistance on request), or

    (b) section 48 (advice on trading scheme regulations),

may give the Committee directions as to the exercise of its functions in responding to that request. If the request is made by two or more national authorities, the directions must be given by them jointly.

(4) The power to give directions under this section does not include power to direct the Committee as to the content of any advice or report.

(5) The power to give directions under this section includes power to vary or revoke the directions.

(6) The Committee must comply with any directions given under this section.

Interpretation

43. Interpretation of Part 2.

Expressions used in this Part that are defined in Part 1 (carbon target and budgeting) have the same meaning as in that Part.

Interpretation of Part 2

43. Interpretation of Part 2.

Expressions used in this Part that are defined in Part 1 (carbon target and budgeting) have the same meaning as in that Part.

Part 3. Trading schemes

Part 3. Trading schemes

44. Trading schemes

(1) The relevant national authority may make provision by regulations for trading schemes relating to greenhouse gas emissions.

(2) A "trading scheme" is a scheme that operates by—

(a) limiting or encouraging the limitation of activities that consist of the emission of greenhouse gas or that cause or contribute, directly or indirectly, to such emissions, or

(b) encouraging activities that consist of, or that cause or contribute, directly or indirectly, to reductions in greenhouse gas emissions or the removal of greenhouse gas from the atmosphere.

45. Activities to which trading schemes may apply

(1) For the purposes of this Part activities are regarded as indirectly causing or contributing to greenhouse gas emissions if they involve, in particular—

(a) the consumption of energy,

(b) the use of materials in whose production energy was consumed,

(c) the disposal otherwise than for recycling of materials in whose production energy was consumed, or

(d) the production or supply of anything whose subsequent use directly causes or contributes to greenhouse gas emissions.

(2) Correspondingly, for the purposes of this Part activities are regarded as indirectly causing or contributing to the reduction of greenhouse gas emissions if they involve a reduction under any of those heads.

(3) This Part applies to activities carried on in the United Kingdom, regardless of where the related emissions, reductions or removals of greenhouse gas occur.

46. Matters that may or must be provided for in regulations

(1) Schedule 2 specifies matters that may or must be provided for in regulations under section 44.

(2) In that Schedule—

Part 1 deals with schemes that operate by limiting or encouraging the limitation of activities that consist of the emission of greenhouse gas or that cause or contribute, directly or indirectly, to such emissions;

Part 2 deals with schemes that operate by encouraging activities that consist of, or that cause or contribute, directly or indirectly, to reductions in greenhouse gas emissions or the removal of greenhouse gas from the atmosphere;

Part 3 deals with administration and enforcement.

(3) Regulations under section 44 may also make provision about the application of the regulations to the Crown.

Authorities and regulations

47. Relevant national authorities

(1) This section identifies "the relevant national authority" for the purposes of this Part.

(2) The Scottish Ministers are the relevant national authority in relation to matters within the legislative competence of the Scottish Parliament.

(3) The Welsh Ministers are the relevant national authority in relation to matters that—

(a) are within the legislative competence of the National Assembly for Wales, or

(b) relate to limiting or encouraging the limitation of activities in Wales that consist of the emission of greenhouse gas, other than activities in connection with offshore oil and gas exploration and exploitation.

(4) In subsection (3)(b)—

"Wales" has the same meaning as in the Government of Wales Act 2006 (c. 32); and "offshore oil and gas exploration and exploitation" has the same meaning as in the National Assembly for Wales (Transfer of Functions) Order 2005 (S.I. 2005/1958).

(5) The Secretary of State or the relevant Northern Ireland department is the relevant authority in relation to reserved matters within the meaning of the Northern Ireland Act 1998 (c. 47).

(6) The relevant Northern Ireland department is the relevant authority in relation to all other matters within the legislative competence of the Northern Ireland Assembly.

(7) The Secretary of State is the relevant national authority in relation to all other matters.

48. Procedure for making regulations

(1) Before making regulations under this Part, a national authority must—

    (a) obtain, and take into account, the advice of the Committee on Climate Change, and

    (b) consult such persons likely to be affected by the regulations as the authority considers appropriate.

(2) In particular, before making regulations under this Part that set a limit on the total amount of the activities to which a trading scheme applies for a trading period or periods, a national authority must obtain, and take into account, the advice of the Committee on Climate Change on the amount of that limit.

(3) Regulations under this Part are subject to affirmative resolution procedure if they contain provision—

    (a) setting up a trading scheme,

    (b) extending the class of participants or activities to which a trading scheme applies,

    (c) extending the duration of a trading scheme,

    (d) making the overall requirements of a trading scheme significantly more onerous,

    (e) conferring new powers to enforce the requirements of a trading scheme,

    (f) imposing or providing for the imposition of new financial or other penalties or increasing the amount of existing financial penalties,

    (g) creating an offence or increasing the penalties for an existing offence, or

    (h) amending or repealing a provision of an enactment contained in primary legislation.

(4) Regulations under this Part are subject to affirmative resolution procedure if they are the first such regulations to contain provision under paragraph 31 of Schedule 2 (appeals).

(5) Other regulations under this Part are subject to negative resolution procedure.

(6) The relevant Northern Ireland department may only make regulations under this Part dealing with a reserved matter within the meaning of the Northern Ireland Act 1998 (c. 47) with the consent of the Secretary of State.

49. Further provisions about regulations

(1) Schedule 3 makes further provision about regulations under this Part.

(2) In that Schedule—

Part 1 relates to regulations made by a single national authority;

Part 2 relates to regulations made by two or more national authorities; and

Part 3 confers power to make provision by Order in Council.

Other supplementary provisions

50. Information

(1) Schedule 4 confers powers to require information for the purposes of enabling a trading scheme to be established.

(2) Paragraphs 1 to 5 of that Schedule shall cease to have effect on 1st January 2011.

51. Powers to give guidance

(1) The relevant national authority may give guidance to the administrator of a trading scheme.

(2) The power to give guidance under this section includes power to vary or revoke it.

(3) The administrator must have regard to any guidance given under this section.

52. Powers to give directions

(1) The relevant national authority may give directions to the administrator of a trading scheme.

(2) The power to give directions under this section includes power to vary or revoke the directions.

(3) The administrator must comply with any directions given under this section.

53. Grants to administrators and participants

(1) A national authority may make, or arrange for the making of, grants to—

    (a) the administrator of a trading scheme, or

    (b) the participants in a trading scheme.

(2) A grant under this section may be made subject to such conditions as may be determined by, or in accordance with arrangements made by, the national authority that makes the grant.

54. Power to make consequential provision

A national authority may by regulations—

    (a) make such provision amending, repealing or revoking any enactment as the authority considers appropriate in consequence of provision made by that authority by regulations under section 44 (trading schemes);

    (b) make such transitional provision and savings as the authority considers appropriate in connection with the coming into effect of such provision.

Interpretation

55. Interpretation of Part 3.

In this Part—

"administrator", in relation to a trading scheme, means a person appointed as the administrator of the scheme by regulations under paragraph 21 of Schedule 2;

"participant", in relation to a trading scheme, means a person to whom the scheme applies by virtue of regulations under paragraph 4 or 15 of Schedule 2;

"trading period", in relation to a trading scheme, means a period by reference to which the scheme is to operate by virtue of regulations under paragraph 2 or 13 of Schedule 2.

Interpretation of Part 3

55. Interpretation of Part 3.

In this Part—

"administrator", in relation to a trading scheme, means a person appointed as the administrator of the scheme by regulations under paragraph 21 of Schedule 2;

"participant", in relation to a trading scheme, means a person to whom the scheme applies by virtue of regulations under paragraph 4 or 15 of Schedule 2;

"trading period", in relation to a trading scheme, means a period by reference to which the scheme is to operate by virtue of regulations under paragraph 2 or 13 of Schedule 2.

Part 4. Impact of and adaptation to climate change

Part 4. Impact of and adaptation to climate change

56. Report on impact of climate change

(1) It is the duty of the Secretary of State to lay reports before Parliament containing an assessment of the risks for the United Kingdom of the current and predicted impact of climate change.

(2) The first report under this section must be laid before Parliament no later than three years after this section comes into force.

(3) Subsequent reports must be laid before Parliament no later than five years after the previous report was so laid.

(4) The Secretary of State may extend the period for laying any such report, but must publish a statement setting out the reasons for the delay and specifying when the report will be laid before Parliament.

(5) Before laying a report under this section before Parliament, the Secretary of State must take into account the advice of the Committee on Climate Change under section 57.

(6) The Secretary of State must send a copy of each report under this section to the other national authorities.

57. Advice of Committee on Climate Change on impact report

(1) It is the duty of the Committee on Climate Change to advise the Secretary of State on the preparation of each of the Secretary of State's reports under section 56.

(2) The Committee must give its advice under this section in relation to a report not later than six months before the last date for laying the report before Parliament (see subsections (2) to (4) of section 56).

(3) The Committee must, at the time it gives its advice under this section to the Secretary of State, send a copy to the other national authorities.

(4) As soon as is reasonably practicable after giving its advice under this section the Committee must publish that advice in such manner as it considers appropriate.

58. Programme for adaptation to climate change

(1) It is the duty of the Secretary of State to lay programmes before Parliament setting out —
    (a) the objectives of Her Majesty's Government in the United Kingdom in relation to adaptation

to climate change,

    (b) the Government's proposals and policies for meeting those objectives, and

    (c) the time-scales for introducing those proposals and policies,

addressing the risks identified in the most recent report under section 56.

(2) The objectives, proposals and policies must be such as to contribute to sustainable development.

(3) Each programme under this section must be laid before Parliament as soon as is reasonably practicable after the laying of the report under section 56 to which it relates.

(4) The Secretary of State must send a copy of each programme under this section to the other national authorities.

59. Reporting on progress in connection with adaptation

(1) Each report of the Committee on Climate Change under section 36 to which this section applies must contain an assessment of the progress made towards implementing the objectives, proposals and policies set out in the programmes laid before Parliament under section 58 (adaptation to climate change).

(2) This section applies to the report in the second year after that in which the Secretary of State lays the first programme under section 58 before Parliament.

(3) After that, this section applies to the report under section 36 in every second year after that in which the Committee last made a report to which this section applies, subject to any order under subsection (4).

(4) The Secretary of State may by order provide that this section shall apply to the report under section 36 in the year specified in the order and in every subsequent year.

(5) An order under subsection (4) is subject to negative resolution procedure.

60. Programme for adaptation to climate change: Northern Ireland

(1) It is the duty of the relevant Northern Ireland department to lay programmes before the Northern Ireland Assembly setting out—

    (a) the objectives of the department in relation to adaptation to climate change,

    (b) the department's proposals and policies for meeting those objectives, and

    (c) the time-scales for introducing those proposals and policies,

addressing the risks identified in the most recent report under section 56.

(2) The objectives, proposals and policies must be such as to contribute to sustainable development.

(3) The second and each subsequent programme under this section must contain an assessment of the progress made towards implementing the objectives, proposals and policies set out in earlier programmes.

(4) Each programme under this section must be laid before the Northern Ireland Assembly as soon as is reasonably practicable after the laying before Parliament of the report under section 56 to which it relates.

(5) The relevant Northern Ireland department must send a copy of each programme under this section to the other national authorities.

Reporting authorities: non-devolved functions

61. Guidance by Secretary of State to reporting authorities

(1) The Secretary of State may issue guidance to reporting authorities about—

(a) assessing the current and predicted impact of climate change in relation to the authorities' functions,

(b) preparing proposals and policies for adapting to climate change in the exercise of their functions, and

(c) co-operating with other reporting authorities for that purpose.

(2) This section does not apply to devolved functions.

62. Directions by Secretary of State to prepare reports

(1) The Secretary of State may direct a reporting authority to prepare a report containing any of the following—

(a) an assessment of the current and predicted impact of climate change in relation to the authority's functions;

(b) a statement of the authority's proposals and policies for adapting to climate change in the exercise of its functions and the time-scales for introducing those proposals and policies;

(c) an assessment of the progress made by the authority towards implementing the proposals and policies set out in its previous reports.

(2) The Secretary of State may direct two or more reporting authorities to prepare a joint report.

(3) The Secretary of State may give directions about—

(a) the time within which a report must be prepared, and

(b) its content,

and may, in particular, require it to cover a particular geographical area.

(4) This section does not apply to devolved functions.

63. Compliance with Secretary of State's directions

(1) A reporting authority must comply with any directions under section 62.

(2) Where two or more reporting authorities are directed to prepare a joint report, they must take reasonable steps to co-operate with each other for that purpose.

(3) In preparing a report, a reporting authority must have regard to the following, so far as relevant—

(a) the most recent report under section 56 (report on impact of climate change);

(b) the most recent programme under section 58 (programme for adaptation to climate change);

(c) any guidance issued by the Secretary of State under section 61.

(4) If the authority—

(a) has functions that are exercisable in or as regards Wales, or

(b) has devolved Welsh functions,

it must also have regard, so far as relevant, to any guidance issued by the Welsh Ministers under section 66 and the most recent report under section 80 (report on climate change: Wales).

(5) The authority must send a copy of the report to the Secretary of State.

(6) The Secretary of State must publish the report in such manner as the Secretary of State considers appropriate.

(7) This does not require the Secretary of State to publish—

(a) information the Secretary of State could refuse to disclose in response to a request under—

(i) the Freedom of Information Act 2000 (c. 36), or

(ii) the Environmental Information Regulations 2004 (S.I. 2004/3391) or any regulations replacing those regulations;

(b) information whose disclosure is prohibited by any enactment.

(8) The authority must have regard to the report in exercising its functions other than its devolved functions.

64. Consent of, or consultation with, devolved authorities

(1) The Secretary of State must obtain the consent of a devolved authority before issuing guidance under section 61 or giving a direction under section 62 relating to functions in relation to which—

(a) functions are exercisable jointly by that devolved authority and a Minister of the Crown, or

(b) functions are exercisable by a Minister of the Crown only with the agreement of that devolved authority.

(2) The Secretary of State must consult a devolved authority before issuing guidance under section 61 or giving a direction under section 62 relating to functions in relation to which—

(a) functions are exercisable by that devolved authority other than jointly with a Minister of the Crown, or

(b) functions are exercisable by a Minister of the Crown only after consultation with that devolved authority.

65. Report on exercise of power to give directions

(1) It is the duty of the Secretary of State to lay reports before Parliament setting out how the Secretary of State intends to exercise the power under section 62 to give directions to reporting authorities.

(2) The reports must, in particular, identify—

(a) the circumstances in which directions are likely to be given, and

(b) the authorities or kinds of authority to whom the Secretary of State considers directions should be given as a matter of priority.

(3) Nothing in a report under this section affects the exercise of the Secretary of State's power under section 62.

(4) Before laying a report under this section before Parliament the Secretary of State must consult such persons likely to be affected by the report as the Secretary of State considers appropriate.

(5) The first report under this section must be laid before Parliament no later than 12 months after this Act is passed.

(6) Subsequent reports must be laid before Parliament no later than the time when the next programme under section 58 is so laid.

(7) The Secretary of State must send a copy of each report under this section to the other national authorities.

Reporting authorities: devolved Welsh functions

66. Guidance by Welsh Ministers to reporting authorities

The Welsh Ministers may issue guidance to reporting authorities about—

(a) assessing the current and predicted impact of climate change in relation to the authorities' devolved Welsh functions,

(b) preparing proposals and policies for adapting to climate change in the exercise of those functions, and

(c) co-operating with other reporting authorities for that purpose.

67. Directions by Welsh Ministers to prepare reports

(1) The Welsh Ministers may direct a reporting authority to prepare a report containing any of the following—

(a) an assessment of the current and predicted impact of climate change in relation to the authority's devolved Welsh functions;

(b) a statement of the authority's proposals and policies for adapting to climate change in the exercise of those functions and the time-scales for introducing those proposals and policies;

(c) an assessment of the progress made by the authority towards implementing the proposals and policies set out in its previous reports.

(2) The Welsh Ministers may direct two or more reporting authorities to prepare a joint report.

(3) The Welsh Ministers may give directions about—

(a) the time within which a report must be prepared, and

(b) its content,

and may, in particular, require it to cover a particular geographical area.

68. Compliance with Welsh Ministers' directions

(1) A reporting authority must comply with any directions under section 67.

(2) Where two or more reporting authorities are directed to prepare a joint report, they must take reasonable steps to co-operate with each other for that purpose.

(3) In preparing a report, a reporting authority must have regard to the following, so far as relevant—

(a) the most recent report under section 56 (report on impact of climate change);

(b) the most recent programme under section 58 (programme for adaptation to climate change);

(c) any guidance issued by the Secretary of State under section 61;

(d) any guidance issued by the Welsh Ministers under section 66;

(e) the most recent report under section 80 (report on climate change: Wales).

(4) The authority must send a copy of the report to the Welsh Ministers.

(5) The Welsh Ministers must publish the report in such manner as they consider appropriate.

(6) This does not require the Welsh Ministers to publish—

(a) information they could refuse to disclose in response to a request under—

(i) the Freedom of Information Act 2000 (c. 36), or

(ii) the Environmental Information Regulations 2004 (S.I. 2004/3391) or any regulations replacing those regulations;

(b) information whose disclosure is prohibited by any enactment.

(7) The authority must have regard to the report in exercising its devolved Welsh functions.

69. Consent of, or consultation with, Secretary of State

(1) The Welsh Ministers must obtain the consent of the Secretary of State before issuing guidance under section 66 or giving a direction under section 67 relating to functions in relation to which—

(a) functions are exercisable by a Minister of the Crown jointly with the Welsh Ministers, the First Minister or the Counsel General, or

(b) functions are exercisable by the Welsh Ministers, the First Minister or the Counsel General only with the agreement of a Minister of the Crown.

(2) The Welsh Ministers must consult the Secretary of State before issuing guidance under section 66 or giving a direction under section 67 relating to functions in relation to which—

(a) functions are exercisable by a Minister of the Crown other than jointly with the Welsh Ministers, the First Minister or the Counsel General, or

(b) functions are exercisable by the Welsh Ministers, the First Minister or the Counsel General only after consultation with a Minister of the Crown.

Interpretation

70. Interpretation

(1) In sections 61 to 69 and this section "reporting authority" means—

(a) a person or body with functions of a public nature,

(b) a person who is or is deemed to be a statutory undertaker for the purposes of any provision of—

(i) Part 11 of the Town and Country Planning Act 1990 (c. 8) (see section 262 of that Act), or

(ii) Part 10 of the Town and Country Planning (Scotland) Act 1997 (c. 8) (see section 214 of that Act), or

(c) a person who is a statutory undertaker within the meaning of [F1the Planning Act (Northern Ireland) 2011 (see section 250 of that Act)].

(2) None of the following are reporting authorities for the purposes of those sections and this section—

(a) a Minister of the Crown;

(b) either House of Parliament;

(c) a devolved authority;

(d) a devolved legislature.

(3) In those sections and this section "devolved authority" means—

(a) the Welsh Ministers, the First Minister or the Counsel General,

(b) the Scottish Ministers, the First Minister, the Lord Advocate or the Solicitor General for Scotland, or

(c) a Minister within the meaning of the Northern Ireland Act 1998 (c. 47) or a Northern Ireland department.

(4) References in those sections to a reporting authority's "devolved functions" are to functions—

(a) conferred or imposed by or under a Measure or Act of the National Assembly for Wales,

(b) exercisable in or as regards Wales and relating to matters within the legislative competence of the National Assembly for Wales,

(c) exercisable in or as regards Scotland and relating to matters within the legislative competence of the Scottish Parliament,

(d) exercisable in or as regards Northern Ireland and relating to transferred matters within the meaning of the Northern Ireland Act 1998, or

(e) in relation to which functions are exercisable by a devolved authority,

and in relation to which no functions are exercisable by a Minister of the Crown.

(5) For this purpose functions are not to be regarded as exercisable by a Minister of the Crown in relation to a reporting authority's functions merely because—

(a) the Minister of the Crown may exercise functions—

(i) under section 2. (2) of the European Communities Act 1972 (c. 68),

(ii) by virtue of section 57. (1) or under section 58 of the Scotland Act 1998 (c. 46) (Community and international obligations),

(iii) under section 27 or 28 of the Northern Ireland Act 1998 (international etc obligations),

(iv) by virtue of paragraph 5 of Schedule 3 to the Government of Wales Act 2006 (c. 32) or under section 82 of that Act (Community and international obligations), or

(v) under section 152 of that Act (intervention in case of functions relating to water etc),

in relation to the reporting authority's functions,

(b) the Minister of the Crown's agreement is required to the exercise of a function by a devolved authority in relation to the reporting authority's functions, or

(c) the Minister of the Crown must be consulted by a devolved authority about the exercise of a function in relation to the reporting authority's functions.

(6) References in those sections to a reporting authority's "devolved Welsh functions" are to functions—

(a) conferred or imposed by or under a Measure or Act of the National Assembly for Wales,

(b) exercisable in or as regards Wales and relating to matters within the legislative competence of the National Assembly for Wales, or

(c) in relation to which functions are exercisable by the Welsh Ministers, the First Minister or the Counsel General.

(7) For this purpose functions are not to be regarded as exercisable by the Welsh Ministers, the First Minister or the Counsel General in relation to a reporting authority's functions merely because—

(a) the agreement of the Welsh Ministers, the First Minister or the Counsel General is required to the exercise of a function by a Minister of the Crown in relation to the reporting authority's functions, or

(b) the Welsh Ministers, the First Minister or the Counsel General must be consulted by a Minister of the Crown about the exercise of a function in relation to the reporting authority's functions.

(8) In those sections and this section—

(a) "Counsel General" and "Wales" have the same meanings as in the Government of Wales Act 2006 (c. 32);

(b) "Minister of the Crown" includes a government department.

Amendments (Textual)

F1. Words in s. 70. (1)(c) substituted (N.I.) (1.4.2015) by Planning Act (Northern-Ireland) 2011 (c. 25), s. 254. (1)(2), Sch. 6 para. 102 (with s. 211); S.R. 2015/49, art. 3, Sch. 1 (with Sch. 2)

Part 5. Other provisions

Part 5. Other provisions

71. Waste reduction schemes

F1. (1). . . . .

F2. (2). . . . .

F2. (3). . . . .

. . . .

Amendments (Textual)

F1. S. 71. (1) repealed (15.1.2012) by Localism Act 2011 (c. 20), ss. 47. (a), 240. (1)(e), Sch. 25 Pt. 8

F2. S. 71. (2)(3) repealed (15.1.2012) by Localism Act 2011 (c. 20), ss. 47. (b), 240. (1)(e), (3)Sch. 25 Pt. 8

F372. Waste reduction provisions: piloting

. . . .

Amendments (Textual)

F3. Ss. 72-75 repealed (15.1.2012) by Localism Act 2011 (c. 20), ss. 47. (b), 240. (1)(e), Sch. 25 Pts. 8

F373. Waste reduction provisions: report and review

. . . .

Amendments (Textual)

F3. Ss. 72-75 repealed (15.1.2012) by Localism Act 2011 (c. 20), ss. 47. (b), 240. (1)(e), Sch. 25

F374. Waste reduction provisions: interim report

. . . .

Amendments (Textual)
F3. Ss. 72-75 repealed (15.1.2012) by Localism Act 2011 (c. 20), ss. 47. (b), 240. (1)(e), Sch. 25
Pts. 8

F375. Waste reduction provisions: roll-out or repeal

. . . .

Amendments (Textual)
F3. Ss. 72-75 repealed (15.1.2012) by Localism Act 2011 (c. 20), ss. 47. (b), 240. (1)(e), Sch. 25
Pts. 8

Collection of household waste

76. Collection of household waste

In section 46 of the Environmental Protection Act 1990 (c. 43) (receptacles for household waste),
after subsection (10) insert—
"(11)A waste collection authority is not obliged to collect household waste that is placed for
collection in contravention of a requirement under this section.".

Charges for [F4single use carrier bags][F4carrier bags]+N.I.

Amendments (Textual)
F4. Words in Sch. 6 para. 2 substituted (N.I.) (28.4.2014) by Carrier Bags Act (Northern Ireland)
2014 (c. 7), s. 1. (b)

77. Charges for [F4single use carrier bags][F4carrier bags]+N.I.

(1) Schedule 6 makes provision about charges for [F4single use carrier bags][F4carrier bags].
(2) In that Schedule—
Part 1 confers power on the relevant national authority to make regulations about charges for
[F4single use carrier bags][F4carrier bags];
Part 2 makes provision about civil sanctions;
Part 3 makes provision about the procedures applying to regulations under the Schedule.
(3) In that Schedule "the relevant national authority" means—
    (a) the Secretary of State in relation to England;
    (b) the Welsh Ministers in relation to Wales;
    (c) the Department of the Environment in Northern Ireland in relation to Northern Ireland.
(4) Regulations under that Schedule are subject to affirmative resolution procedure if—
    (a) they are the first regulations to be made by the relevant national authority in question under
the Schedule,
    [F5. (aa)they are the first regulations to be made by the Welsh Ministers under paragraph 4. A
of the Schedule,]
    [F6. (aa)they are to be made by the Department of the Environment in Northern Ireland under

paragraph 4. A of the Schedule;]

[F7. (ab)they are to be made by the Department of the Environment in Northern Ireland and increase the minimum amount specified under paragraph 4 of the Schedule;]

(b) they contain provision imposing or providing for the imposition of new civil sanctions,

(c) they increase the amount or maximum amount of a monetary penalty or change the basis on which such an amount or maximum is to be determined, or

(d) they amend or repeal a provision of an enactment contained in primary legislation.

(5) Otherwise regulations under that Schedule are subject to negative resolution procedure.

[F8. (6)Section 17. (5) of the Interpretation Act (Northern Ireland) 1954 applies to a power to make regulations under Schedule 6.]

Amendments (Textual)

F5. S. 77. (4)(aa) inserted (E.W.) (15.2.2011) by Waste (Wales) Measure 2010 (nawm 8), ss. 2, 21. (2)

F6. S. 77. (4)(aa) inserted (N.I.) (4.5.2011) by Single Use Carrier Bags Act (Northern Ireland) 2011 (c. 26), s. 1. (2)

F7. S. 77. (6) inserted (N.I.) (28.4.2014) by Carrier Bags Act (Northern Ireland) 2014 (c. 7), s. 2. (3)

F8. S. 77. (4)(ab) inserted (N.I.) (28.4.2014) by Carrier Bags Act (Northern Ireland) 2014 (c. 7), s. 2. (2)

Renewable transport fuel obligations

78. Renewable transport fuel obligations

Schedule 7 contains amendments to the provisions of the Energy Act 2004 (c. 20) relating to renewable transport fuel obligations.

Carbon emissions reduction targets

79. Carbon emissions reduction targets

Schedule 8 contains amendments to the provisions of the Gas Act 1986 (c. 44), the Electricity Act 1989 (c. 29) and the Utilities Act 2000 (c. 27) relating to carbon emissions reduction targets.

Miscellaneous

80. Report on climate change: Wales

(1) It is the duty of the Welsh Ministers to lay before the National Assembly for Wales from time to time a report on—

(a) the objectives of the Welsh Ministers in relation to greenhouse gas emissions and the impact of climate change in Wales,

(b) the action that has been taken by the Welsh Ministers and others to deal with such emissions and that impact, and

(c) the future priorities for the Welsh Ministers and others for dealing with such emissions and that impact.

(2) The report must, in particular, set out how the Welsh Ministers intend to exercise the power to

give directions under section 67 (directions to reporting authorities to prepare adaptation reports).

(3) Nothing in a report under this section affects the exercise of the Welsh Ministers' power under that section.

(4) The second and each subsequent report under this section must contain an assessment of the progress made towards implementing the objectives mentioned in the earlier reports.

(5) In this section "Wales" has the same meaning as in the Government of Wales Act 2006 (c. 32).

Prospective

81. Climate change measures reports in Wales

(1) The Climate Change and Sustainable Energy Act 2006 (c. 19) is amended as follows.

(2) After section 3 insert—

"3. ALocal authorities in Wales to have regard to climate change measures reports

(1) The Welsh Ministers must from time to time publish a climate change measures report.

(2) A local authority in Wales must, in exercising its functions, have regard to any current climate change measures report.

(3) A "climate change measures report" means a report containing information about the local authority measures the Welsh Ministers consider would or might have any of the following effects—

(a) improving efficiency in the use of any description or source of energy;

(b) increasing the amount of energy generated, or heat produced, by microgeneration;

(c) increasing the amount of energy generated, or heat produced, by plant that relies wholly or mainly on a source of energy or a technology listed in section 26. (2);

(d) reducing emissions of greenhouse gases;

(e) reducing the number of households in which one or more persons are living in fuel poverty;

(f) addressing the impact of climate change.

(4) Before publishing a climate change measures report, the Welsh Ministers must consult such representatives of local government, and such other persons, as the Welsh Ministers consider appropriate.

(5) The Secretary of State's consent is required to the publication in a climate change measures report of information about a local authority measure to which subsection (6) applies.

(6) This subsection applies to a local authority measure if the Secretary of State has a function in relation to the measure of—

(a) making subordinate legislation,

(b) issuing guidance or directions, or

(c) making determinations or hearing appeals,

and that function is exercisable in relation to Wales.

(7) In this section—

"local authority" means any of the following—

- a county council;

- a county borough council;

- a community council;

"local authority measure" means anything a local authority in Wales may do in the exercise of its functions (including deciding not to exercise a power).".

F9. (3). . . . .

Amendments (Textual)

F9. S. 81. (3) omitted (26.5.2015) by virtue of Deregulation Act 2015 (c. 20), ss. 57. (4)(b), 115. (3)(e)

82. Repeal of previous reporting obligation

Section 2 of the Climate Change and Sustainable Energy Act 2006 (c. 19) (annual report on greenhouse gas emissions) is repealed.

83. Guidance on reporting

(1) The Secretary of State must publish guidance on the measurement or calculation of greenhouse gas emissions to assist the reporting by persons on such emissions from activities for which they are responsible.

(2) The guidance must be published not later than 1st October 2009.

(3) The Secretary of State may from time to time publish revisions to guidance under this section or revised guidance.

(4) Before publishing guidance under this section or revisions to it, the Secretary of State must consult the other national authorities.

(5) Guidance under this section and revisions to it may be published in such manner as the Secretary of State thinks fit.

84. Report on contribution of reporting to climate change objectives

(1) The Secretary of State must—

(a) review the contribution that reporting on greenhouse gas emissions may make to the achievement of the objectives of Her Majesty's Government in the United Kingdom in relation to climate change, and

(b) lay a report before Parliament setting out the conclusions of that review.

(2) The report must be laid before Parliament not later than 1st December 2010.

(3) In complying with this section the Secretary of State must consult the other national authorities.

85. Regulations about reporting by companies

(1) The Secretary of State must, not later than 6th April 2012—

(a) make regulations under section 416. (4) of the Companies Act 2006 (c. 46) requiring the directors' report of a company to contain such information as may be specified in the regulations about emissions of greenhouse gases from activities for which the company is responsible, or

(b) lay before Parliament a report explaining why no such regulations have been made.

(2) Subsection (1)(a) is complied with if regulations are made containing provision in relation to companies, and emissions, of a description specified in the regulations.

86. Report on the civil estate

(1) It is the duty of the [F10. Minister for the Cabinet Office] to lay before Parliament in respect of each year, beginning with the year 2008, a report containing an assessment of the progress made in the year towards improving the efficiency and contribution to sustainability of buildings that are part of the civil estate.

(2) The report must, in particular, include an assessment of the progress made in the year to which it relates towards—

(a) reducing the size of the civil estate, and

(b) ensuring that buildings that become part of the civil estate fall within the top quartile of energy performance.

(3) If a building that does not fall within the top quartile of energy performance becomes part of the civil estate in the year to which the report relates, the report must state the reasons why the building has nevertheless become part of the civil estate.

(4) A report under this section must be laid before Parliament not later than 1st June in the year following the year to which it relates.

(5) In this section "building" means a building that uses energy for heating or cooling the whole or any part of its interior.

(6) For the purposes of this section, a building is part of the civil estate if it is—

(a) used for the purposes of central government administration, and

(b) of a description of buildings for which, at the passing of this Act, the Treasury has responsibilities in relation to efficiency and sustainability.

(7) The [F11. Minister for the Cabinet Office] may by order provide for buildings of a specified description to be treated as being, or as not being, part of the civil estate for the purposes of this section.

(8) Any such order is subject to affirmative resolution procedure.

Amendments (Textual)

F10. Words in s. 86. (1) substituted (13.4.2011) by The Transfer of Functions (Report on the Civil Estate) Order 2011 (S.I. 2011/740), arts. 1. (2), 3

F11. Words in s. 86. (7) substituted (13.4.2011) by The Transfer of Functions (Report on the Civil Estate) Order 2011 (S.I. 2011/740), arts. 1. (2), 3

Modifications etc. (not altering text)

C1. S. 86 transfer of functions (13.4.2011) by The Transfer of Functions (Report on the Civil Estate) Order 2011 (S.I. 2011/740), arts. 1. (2), 2

87. Power of Ministers and departments to offset greenhouse gas emissions

(1) An authority to which this section applies may acquire and dispose of units or interests in units representing—

(a) a reduction in an amount of greenhouse gas emissions,

(b) the removal of an amount of greenhouse gas from the atmosphere, or

(c) an amount of greenhouse gas emissions allowed under a scheme or arrangement imposing a limit on such emissions.

(2) This section applies to—

(a) any Minister of the Crown or government department;

(b) the Scottish Ministers;

(c) the Welsh Ministers;

(d) any Northern Ireland department.

(3) If the Treasury acquire such units or interests in units, until they are disposed of they shall be treated as held by the persons for the time being constituting the Treasury.

88. Fines for offences relating to pollution

(1) In section 105. (2) of the Clean Neighbourhoods and Environment Act 2005 (c. 16) (which postpones the increase by subsection (1)(b) in maximum fines under regulations under the Pollution Prevention and Control Act 1999 (c. 24) pending the commencement of section 154. (1) of the Criminal Justice Act 2003 (c. 44)), for "Subsection (1)" substitute " Subsection (1)(a) ".

F12. (2). . . . .

Amendments (Textual)

F12. S. 88. (2) repealed (6.4.2010) by The Environmental Permitting (England and Wales) Regulations 2010 (S.I. 2010/675), reg. 1. (1)(b), Sch. 28 (with reg. 1. (2), Sch. 4)

Part 6. General supplementary provisions

Part 6. General supplementary provisions

89. Territorial scope of provisions relating to greenhouse gas emissions

(1) The provisions of this Act relating to emissions of greenhouse gases apply to emissions from sources or other matters occurring in, above or below—
  (a) UK coastal waters, or
  (b) the UK sector of the continental shelf,
as they apply to emissions from sources or matters occurring in the United Kingdom.
(2) In subsection (1)—
"UK coastal waters" means areas landward of the seaward limit of the territorial sea adjacent to the United Kingdom;
"the UK sector of the continental shelf" means the areas designated under section 1. (7) of the Continental Shelf Act 1964 (c. 29).
(3) This section is subject to section 30 (emissions from international aviation or international shipping not to count as emissions from UK sources for the purposes of Part 1, except as provided by regulations).

Orders and regulations

90. Orders and regulations

(1) Orders and regulations under this Act must be made by statutory instrument, subject as follows.
(2) The power of a Northern Ireland department to make regulations under Part 3 (trading schemes) or Schedule 6 (charges for [F1single use carrier bags][F1carrier bags])—
  (a) is exercisable by statutory instrument if the instrument also contains regulations under that Part or Schedule made or to be made by another national authority, and
  (b) otherwise, is exercisable by statutory rule for the purposes of the Statutory Rules (Northern Ireland) Order 1979 (S.I. 1979/1573 (N.I. 12)).
(3) An order or regulations under this Act may—
  (a) make different provision for different cases or circumstances,
  (b) include supplementary, incidental and consequential provision, and
  (c) make transitional provision and savings.
(4) Any provision that may be made by order under this Act may be made by regulations.
(5) Any provision that may be made by regulations under this Act may be made by order.
Amendments (Textual)
F1. Words in Sch. 6 para. 2 substituted (N.I.) (28.4.2014) by Carrier Bags Act (Northern Ireland) 2014 (c. 7), s. 1. (b)

91. Affirmative and negative resolution procedure

(1) Where orders or regulations under this Act are subject to "affirmative resolution procedure" the order or regulations must not be made unless a draft of the statutory instrument containing them has been laid before and approved by a resolution of each House of Parliament.
(2) Where orders or regulations under this Act are subject to "negative resolution procedure" the

statutory instrument containing the order or regulations is subject to annulment in pursuance of a resolution of either House of Parliament.

(3) Any provision that may be made by an order or regulations under this Act subject to negative resolution procedure may be made by an order or regulations subject to affirmative resolution procedure.

(4) This section does not apply to—

(a) regulations under Part 3 (trading schemes) (but see Schedule 3), or

(b) regulations under Schedule 6 (but see Part 3 of that Schedule).

Interpretation

92. Meaning of "greenhouse gas"

(1) In this Act "greenhouse gas" means any of the following—

(a) carbon dioxide (CO_2),

(b) methane (CH_4),

(c) nitrous oxide ($N_2. O$),

(d) hydrofluorocarbons (HFCs),

(e) perfluorocarbons (PFCs),

(f) sulphur hexafluoride (SF_6).

(2) The Secretary of State may by order amend the definition of "greenhouse gas" in subsection (1) to add to the gases listed in that definition.

(3) That power may only be exercised if it appears to the Secretary of State that an agreement or arrangement at European or international level recognises that the gas to be added contributes to climate change.

(4) An order under this section is subject to negative resolution procedure.

93. Measurement of emissions etc by reference to carbon dioxide equivalent

(1) For the purposes of this Act greenhouse gas emissions, reductions of such emissions and removals of greenhouse gas from the atmosphere shall be measured or calculated in tonnes of carbon dioxide equivalent.

(2) A "tonne of carbon dioxide equivalent" means one metric tonne of carbon dioxide or an amount of any other greenhouse gas with an equivalent global warming potential (calculated consistently with international carbon reporting practice).

94. Meaning of "international carbon reporting practice"

(1) In this Act "international carbon reporting practice" means accepted practice in relation to reporting for the purposes of the protocols to the United Nations Framework Convention on Climate Change or such other agreements or arrangements at European or international level as the Secretary of State may specify by order.

(2) An order under this section is subject to negative resolution procedure.

95. Meaning of "national authority"

(1) In this Act "national authority" means any of the following—

(a) the Secretary of State;

(b) the Scottish Ministers;

(c) the Welsh Ministers;

(d) the relevant Northern Ireland department.

(2) Functions conferred or imposed by this Act on "the national authorities" are to be exercised by all of them jointly.

96. Meaning of "relevant Northern Ireland department"

(1) In this Act "the relevant Northern Ireland department", in relation to a matter or provision, means the Northern Ireland department responsible for the matter or, as the case may be, for the matters to which the provision relates.

(2) If more than one department is responsible, the reference is to all of them.

(3) Any question as to the Northern Ireland department responsible for a matter is to be determined by the Department of Finance and Personnel in Northern Ireland.

97. Minor definitions

In this Act—

"devolved legislature" means—

   - the Scottish Parliament,

   - the National Assembly for Wales, or

   - the Northern Ireland Assembly;

"emissions", in relation to a greenhouse gas, means emissions of that gas into the atmosphere that are attributable to human activity;

"enactment" includes—

   - an enactment contained in subordinate legislation within the meaning of the Interpretation Act 1978 (c. 30),

   - an enactment contained in, or in an instrument made under, an Act of the Scottish Parliament,

   - an enactment contained in, or in an instrument made under, Northern Ireland legislation, and

   - an enactment contained in, or in an instrument made under, a Measure or Act of the National Assembly for Wales;

"European law" means—

   - all the rights, powers, liabilities, obligations and restrictions from time to time created or arising by or under the [F2. EU] Treaties, and

   - all the remedies and procedures from time to time provided for by or under the [F2. EU] Treaties,

and "European policy" has a corresponding meaning;

"modifications", in relation to an enactment, includes additions or amendments to, or omissions from, the enactment;

"primary legislation" means—

   - an Act of Parliament,

   - an Act of the Scottish Parliament,

   - a Measure or Act of the National Assembly for Wales, or

   - Northern Ireland legislation.

Amendments (Textual)

F2. Words in Act substituted (22.4.2011) by The Treaty of Lisbon (Changes in Terminology) Order 2011 (S.I. 2011/1043), arts. 2, 3, 6 (with art. 3. (2)(3)4. (2)6. (4)6. (5))

98. Index of defined expressions

In this Act the following expressions are defined or otherwise explained by the provisions indicated—

"the 1990 baseline" (in Parts 1 and 2) | | section 1(2) |

"administrator" (in Part 3) | | section 55 |

"administrator" (in Schedule 6) | | paragraph 6(1) and (4) of Schedule 6 |

"affirmative resolution procedure" (except in Part 3 and Schedule 6) | | section 91(1) |

"annual equivalent", in relation to the carbon budget for a period (in Parts 1 and 2) | | section 5(2) |

"budgetary periods" (in Parts 1 and 2) | | section 4(1) |

"carbon budget" (in Parts 1 and 2) | | section 4(1) |

"carbon unit" (in Parts 1 and 2) | | section 26(1) |

"the chair" (in Schedule 1) | | paragraph 1(1) of Schedule 1 |

[F3 "children" (in Schedule 6)] | | [F3paragraph 4B(2) of Schedule 6] |

"civil sanction" (in Schedule 6) | | paragraph 9(3) of Schedule 6 |

"the Committee" (in Part 2) | | section 32 |

"Counsel General" (in sections 61 to 70) | | section 70(8) |

"the deputy chair" (in Schedule 1) | | paragraph 2 of Schedule 1 |

"devolved authority" (in sections 61 to 70) | | section 70(3) |

"devolved functions", in relation to a reporting authority (in sections 61 to 69) | | section 70(4) and (5) |

"devolved legislature" | | section 97 |

"devolved Welsh functions", in relation to a reporting authority (in sections 61 to 69) | | section 70(6) and (7) |

"discretionary requirement" (in Schedule 6) | | paragraph 12(3) of Schedule 6 |

"electricity distributor" (in Schedule 4) | | paragraph 2(3) of Schedule 4 |

"electricity supplier" (in Schedule 4) | | paragraph 2(2) of Schedule 4 |

"emissions" | | section 97 |

"enactment" | | section 97 |

"environmental authority" (in Schedule 4) | | paragraph 1(2) of Schedule 4 |

"European law" | | section 97 |

"European policy" | | section 97 |

"financial year" (in Schedule 1) | | paragraph 23 of Schedule 1 |

"fixed monetary penalty" (in Schedule 6) | | paragraph 10(3) of Schedule 6 |

"greenhouse gas" | | section 92 |

"international carbon reporting practice" | | section 94 |

"Minister of the Crown" (in sections 61 to 70) | | section 70(8) |

"modifications", in relation to an enactment | | section 97 |

"national authority" | | section 95 |

"negative resolution procedure" (except in Part 3 and Schedule 6) | | section 91(2) |

"net UK carbon account" (in Parts 1 and 2) | | section 27(1) |

"net UK emissions" for a period, in relation to a greenhouse gas (in Parts 1 and 2) | | section 29(1) |

"non-monetary discretionary requirement" (in Schedule 6) | | paragraph 12(4) of Schedule 6 |

[F4 "nuisance" (in Schedule 6)] | | [F4paragraph 4B(6) of Schedule 6] |

"participant" (in Part 3) | | section 55 |

[F5 "pollution" (in Schedule 6)] | | [F5paragraph 4B(3) of Schedule 6] |

"potential participant" (in Schedule 4) | | paragraph 3(2) of Schedule 4 |

"primary legislation" | | section 97 |

"the relevant national authority" (in Part 3) | | section 47 |

"the relevant national authority" (in Schedule 6) | | section 77(3) |

"the relevant Northern Ireland department" | | section 96 |

"reporting authority" (in sections 61 to 70) | | section 70(1) and (2) |

"seller" (in Schedule 6) | | paragraph 3 of Schedule 6 |

"[F6single use carrier bag][F6carrier bag]" (in Schedule 6) | | paragraph 5 of Schedule 6 |

"specified" (in Schedule 6) | | paragraph 3(4) of Schedule 6 |
"targeted greenhouse gas" (in Parts 1 and 2) | | section 24(1) |
"trading period" (in Part 3) | | section 55 |
"trading scheme" | | section 44(2) |
"UK emissions", in relation to a greenhouse gas (in Part 1) | | section 29(1) |
"UK removals", in relation to a greenhouse gas (in Part 1) | | section 29(1) |
"variable monetary penalty" (in Schedule 6) | | paragraph 12(4) of Schedule 6 |
"Wales" (in sections 61 to 70) | | section 70(8) |
F7... | | F7... |
[F8 "young people" (in Schedule 6)] | | [F8paragraph 4B(8) of Schedule 6] |
Amendments (Textual)
F3. Words in s. 98 Table inserted (E.W.) (15.2.2011) by Waste (Wales) Measure 2010 (nawm 8), s. 21. (2), Sch. para. 2. (2)
F4. Words in s. 98 Table inserted (E.W.) (15.2.2011) by Waste (Wales) Measure 2010 (nawm 8), s. 21. (2), Sch. para. 2. (3)
F5. Words in s. 98 Table inserted (E.W.) (15.2.2011) by Waste (Wales) Measure 2010 (nawm 8), s. 21. (2), Sch. para. 2. (4)
F6 Words in Act substituted (N.I.) (28.4.2014) by Carrier Bags Act (Northern Ireland) 2014 (c. 7), s. 1. (a)
F7. S. 98 entry repealed (15.1.2012) by Localism Act 2011 (c. 20), s. 240. (1)(m), Sch. 25 Pt. 8
F8. Words in s. 98 Table inserted (E.W.) (15.2.2011) by Waste (Wales) Measure 2010 (nawm 8), s. 21. (2), Sch. para. 2. (5)

Final provisions

99. Extent

(1) This Act, apart from the provisions listed below, extends to the whole of the United Kingdom.
(2) The following provisions of this Act extend to England and Wales only—
    (a) sections 71 to 75 and Schedule 5 (waste reduction schemes);
    (b) section 76 (collection of household waste);
    (c) section 81 (climate change measures reports in Wales);
    (d) section 88 (fines for offences relating to pollution).
(3) Section 77 and Schedule 6 (charges for [F1single use carrier bags][F1carrier bags]) extend to England and Wales and Northern Ireland only.
(4) Section 79 and Schedule 8 (carbon emissions reduction targets) extend to England and Wales and Scotland only.
Amendments (Textual)
F1. Words in Sch. 6 para. 2 substituted (N.I.) (28.4.2014) by Carrier Bags Act (Northern Ireland) 2014 (c. 7), s. 1. (b)

100. Commencement

(1) Part 1 (carbon target and budgeting), Part 2 (the Committee on Climate Change) and this Part come into force on the day this Act is passed.
(2) Section 71. (1) and Schedule 5 (waste reduction schemes) come into force in accordance with sections 72 to 75.
(3) Section 81 (climate change measures reports in Wales) comes into force on such day as may be appointed by order made by the Welsh Ministers.
(4) Section 82 (repeal of previous reporting obligation) comes into force on 1st January 2009.

(5) The other provisions of this Act come into force at the end of two months beginning with the day it is passed.

101. Short title

The short title of this Act is the Climate Change Act 2008.

Schedules

Schedule 1. The Committee on Climate Change

Section 32

Membership

1. (1)The Committee shall consist of—
(a) a person appointed by the national authorities to chair the Committee ("the chair"), and
(b) not less than five and not more than eight other members appointed by the national authorities.
(2) The national authorities must consult the chair before appointing the other members.
(3) In appointing a member, the national authorities must have regard to the desirability of securing that the Committee (taken as a whole) has experience in or knowledge of the following—
(a) business competitiveness;
(b) climate change policy at national and international level, and in particular the social impacts of such policy;
(c) climate science, and other branches of environmental science;
(d) differences in circumstances between England, Wales, Scotland and Northern Ireland and the capacity of national authorities to take action in relation to climate change;
(e) economic analysis and forecasting;
(f) emissions trading;
(g) energy production and supply;
(h) financial investment;
(i) technology development and diffusion.
(4) The Secretary of State may by order amend sub-paragraph (1)(b) so as to alter the minimum or maximum number of members of the Committee.
(5) Such an order may only be made with the consent of the other national authorities.
(6) Any such order is subject to negative resolution procedure.
2. The national authorities may, after consulting the chair, appoint one of the members as deputy to the chair ("the deputy chair").

Term of office

3. A member holds and vacates office in accordance with the terms of the member's appointment.
4. A member may resign by giving written notice to the Secretary of State.
5. The national authorities may remove a member—
(a) who has been absent from meetings of the Committee without its permission for a period of 6 months or more,
(b) who has become bankrupt or has made an arrangement with creditors,
(c) whose estate has been sequestrated in Scotland or who, under Scots law, has made a

composition or arrangement with, or granted a trust deed for, creditors, or

(d) who in the opinion of the national authorities is otherwise unable or unfit to carry out the duties of that member.

6. A person ceases to be the chair or the deputy chair if the person—

(a) resigns that office by giving written notice to the Secretary of State, or

(b) ceases to be a member.

7. A person who—

(a) ceases to be a member, or

(b) ceases to be the chair or the deputy chair,

may be reappointed to that office.

Remuneration and pensions etc

8. The Committee may pay to the members such remuneration and allowances as the national authorities may determine.

9. The Committee must, if required to do so by the national authorities—

(a) pay such pensions, gratuities or allowances as the national authorities may determine to or in respect of any person who is or has been a member, or

(b) pay such sums as the national authorities may determine towards provision for the payment of pensions, gratuities or allowances to or in respect of such a person.

10. If the national authorities consider there are special circumstances which make it right for a person who has ceased to be a member to receive compensation, the Committee must pay the person such compensation as the national authorities may determine.

Staff

11. (1)The Committee must appoint a person to be chief executive, but may only appoint a person who has been approved by the national authorities.

(2) The chief executive is an employee of the Committee.

12. The Committee may appoint other employees.

13. The Committee must, if required to do so by the national authorities—

(a) pay such pensions, gratuities or allowances as the national authorities may determine to or in respect of any employee or former employee, or

(b) pay such sums as the national authorities may determine towards provision for the payment of pensions, gratuities or allowances to or in respect of any employee or former employee.

14. (1)In Schedule 1 to the Superannuation Act 1972 (c. 11) (kinds of employment to which section 1 of that Act applies), in the list of other bodies, at the appropriate place insert— " The Committee on Climate Change. "

(2) The Committee must pay to the Minister for the Civil Service, at such times as the Minister may direct, such sums as the Minister may determine in respect of any increase attributable to sub-paragraph (1) in the sums payable out of money provided by Parliament under the Superannuation Act 1972.

Sub-committees

15. (1)The Committee may establish sub-committees.

(2) A sub-committee may include persons who are not members of the Committee.

(3) The Committee may pay such remuneration and allowances as the national authorities may determine to any person who—

(a) is a member of a sub-committee, but

(b) is not a member of the Committee.

(4) This paragraph does not apply in relation to the Adaptation Sub-Committee.

The Adaptation Sub-Committee

16. (1)There shall be a sub-committee of the Committee, to be known as the Adaptation Sub-Committee or, in Welsh, as yr Is-bwyllgor Addasu (referred to in this paragraph as "the ASC").
(2) The ASC shall consist of—
(a) a person appointed by the national authorities to chair the ASC ("the ASC chair"), and
(b) not less than five other members appointed by the national authorities.
(3) The national authorities must—
(a) consult the chair before appointing the ASC chair, and
(b) consult the ASC chair before appointing the other members of the ASC.
(4) A person ceases to be the ASC chair if the person—
(a) resigns that office by giving written notice to the Secretary of State, or
(b) ceases to be a member of the ASC.
(5) The ASC may include persons who are not members of the Committee.
(6) Paragraphs 3 to 5 (term of office) apply to a person who is—
(a) a member of the Committee, and
(b) a member of the ASC,
in that person's capacity as a member of the ASC.
(7) Those paragraphs and paragraphs 8 to 10 (remuneration and pensions etc) apply to a member of the ASC who is not a member of the Committee as they apply to a member of the Committee.
(8) In the application of paragraph 5. (a) by virtue of this paragraph, the reference to the Committee is a reference to the ASC.
(9) A person who—
(a) ceases to be a member of the ASC, or
(b) ceases to be the ASC chair,
may be reappointed to that office.
(10) The ASC must provide the Committee with such advice, analysis, information or other assistance as the Committee may require in connection with the exercise of its functions under—
(a) section 38. (1)(c) (advice etc to national authorities on adaptation to climate change),
(b) section 57 (advice on report on impact of climate change), or
(c) section 59 (reporting on progress in connection with adaptation).

Proceedings

17. The Committee may regulate—
(a) its own procedure (including quorum), and
(b) the procedure of any sub-committee (including quorum).
18. The validity of anything done by the Committee or any sub-committee is not affected by—
(a) any vacancy in the membership of the Committee or sub-committee, or
(b) any defect in the appointment of any member of the Committee or sub-committee.
19. The Committee must publish the minutes of its meetings in such manner as it considers appropriate.

Discharge of functions

20. The Committee may authorise a sub-committee, member or employee to exercise any of the Committee's functions.

Application of seal and proof of documents

21. (1)The application of the Committee's seal must be authenticated by the signature of—+N.I.

(a) a member of the Committee who is authorised (generally or specially) for that purpose, or

(b) an employee who is so authorised.

(2) A document purporting to be duly executed under the seal of the Committee or to be signed on behalf of the Committee shall be received in evidence and treated as so executed or signed unless the contrary is shown.

(3) This paragraph does not apply in relation to Scotland.

Reports and accounts

22. (1)For each financial year the Committee must—

(a) prepare an annual report on the discharge of its functions during the year, and

(b) send a copy to the national authorities within such period as the national authorities may direct.

(2) A copy of each report received under this paragraph must be laid—

(a) by the Secretary of State before Parliament,

(b) by the Scottish Ministers before the Scottish Parliament,

(c) by the Welsh Ministers before the National Assembly for Wales, and

(d) by the relevant Northern Ireland department before the Northern Ireland Assembly.

23. In this Schedule "financial year" means—

(a) the period beginning with the day the Committee is established and ending with the next 31st March, and

(b) each subsequent period of 12 months ending with 31st March.

24. (1)The Committee must keep proper accounts and proper records in relation to the accounts.

(2) For each financial year the Committee must—

(a) prepare a statement of accounts in respect of that financial year, and

(b) send a copy of the statement to the national authorities and the Comptroller and Auditor General within such period as the national authorities direct.

(3) The statement must be in such form as the national authorities may direct.

(4) The Comptroller and Auditor General must—

(a) examine, certify and report on the statement, and

(b) send a copy of the certified statement and the report to the national authorities as soon as possible.

(5) A copy of each statement received under sub-paragraph (4) must be laid—

(a) by the Secretary of State before Parliament,

(b) by the Scottish Ministers before the Scottish Parliament,

(c) by the Welsh Ministers before the National Assembly for Wales, and

(d) by the relevant Northern Ireland department before the Northern Ireland Assembly.

Information

25. (1)The Committee must provide the national authorities with such information as they may request about its property.

(2) The Committee must provide the Secretary of State with such information as the Secretary of State may request about the exercise or proposed exercise of its functions under—

(a) Part 1 (carbon target and budgeting),

(b) section 33 (advice on level of 2050 target),

(c) section 34 (advice in connection with carbon budgets),

(d) section 35 (advice on emissions from international aviation and international shipping),

(e) section 36 (reports on progress),

(f) section 57 (advice on report on impact of climate change), or

(g) section 59 (reporting on progress in connection with adaptation).

(3) The Committee must provide a national authority with such information as the national authority may request about the exercise or proposed exercise of the Committee's functions under—

(a) section 38 (duty to provide advice or assistance on request), or

(b) section 48 (advice on trading scheme regulations),

in relation to that national authority.

If the information relates to the exercise or proposed exercise of those functions in relation to two or more national authorities, the request must be made by all of them jointly.

(4) The Committee must provide the national authorities with such information as they may request about the exercise or proposed exercise of any of its other functions.

(5) The Committee must also—

(a) permit any person authorised by a national authority to inspect and make copies of any accounts or other documents of the Committee, and

(b) provide such explanation of them as that person or the national authority may require.

(6) Before exercising a function under sub-paragraph (5), the national authority must consult the other national authorities.

Publication of advice etc

26. A requirement under this Act for the Committee to publish anything does not oblige it to publish—

(a) information it could refuse to disclose in response to a request under—

(i) the Freedom of Information Act 2000 (c. 36), or

(ii) the Environmental Information Regulations 2004 (S.I. 2004/3391) or any regulations replacing those regulations;

(b) information whose disclosure is prohibited by any enactment.

Status

27. (1)The Committee is not to be regarded as the servant or agent of the Crown or as enjoying any status, privilege or immunity of the Crown.

(2) The Committee is to be treated as a cross-border public authority within the meaning of the Scotland Act 1998 (c. 46) for the purposes of the following provisions of that Act—

(a) section 23. (2)(b) (power of Scottish Parliament to require persons outside Scotland to attend to give evidence or produce documents);

(b) section 70. (6) (legislation of Scottish Parliament not to require certain cross-border public authorities to prepare accounts).

Public Records Act 1958 (c. 51)

28. In Schedule 1 to the Public Records Act 1958 (definition of public records), in Part 2 of the Table at the end of paragraph 3, at the appropriate place insert— " The Committee on Climate Change. "

Parliamentary Commissioner Act 1967 (c. 13)

29. In Schedule 2 to the Parliamentary Commissioner Act 1967 (departments etc subject to investigation)—

(a) at the appropriate place insert— " The Committee on Climate Change. ", and

(b) in the notes at the appropriate place insert—

"Committee on Climate Change

In the case of the Committee on Climate Change, no investigation is to be conducted in respect of any action taken by or on behalf of the Committee—

(a) in the exercise in or as regards Scotland of any function to the extent that the function is exercisable within devolved competence (within the meaning of section 54 of the Scotland Act 1998), or

(b) in connection with functions of the Committee in relation to Wales (within the meaning of the Government of Wales Act 2006)."

House of Commons Disqualification Act 1975 (c. 24)

30. In Part 2 of Schedule 1 to the House of Commons Disqualification Act 1975 (bodies of which all members are disqualified), at the appropriate place insert— " The Committee on Climate Change. "

Northern Ireland Assembly Disqualification Act 1975 (c. 25)

31. In Part 2 of Schedule 1 to the Northern Ireland Assembly Disqualification Act 1975 (bodies of which all members are disqualified), at the appropriate place insert— " The Committee on Climate Change. "

Race Relations Act 1976 (c. 74)

32[F1 In Part 2 of Schedule 1. A to the Race Relations Act 1976 (bodies and other persons subject to general statutory duty), at the appropriate place insert— " The Committee on Climate Change. "]

Amendments (Textual)

F1. Sch. 1 para. 32 repealed (E.W.S.) (4.4.2011) by 2010 c. 15, Sch. 27 Pt. 1. A (as inserted by The Equality Act 2010 (Public Authorities and Consequential and Supplementary Amendments) Order 2011 (S.I. 2011/1060), arts. 1. (2), 3. (3)(a), Schs. 3)

Freedom of Information Act 2000 (c. 36)

33. In Part 6 of Schedule 1 to the Freedom of Information Act 2000 (other public bodies and offices which are public authorities), at the appropriate place insert— " The Committee on Climate Change. "

Scottish Public Services Ombudsman Act 2002 (asp 11)

34. (1)The Scottish Public Services Ombudsman Act 2002 is amended as follows.

(2) In section 7 (matters which may be investigated: restrictions), after subsection (6. B) insert—

"(6. C)The Ombudsman must not investigate action taken by or on behalf of the Committee on Climate Change in the exercise in or as regards Scotland of any function to the extent that the function is not exercisable within devolved competence (within the meaning of section 54 of the Scotland Act 1998)."

(3) In Schedule 2 (persons liable to investigation), after paragraph 91. A insert—

"91. BThe Committee on Climate Change."

Public Services Ombudsman (Wales) Act 2005 (c. 10)

35. In Schedule 3 to the Public Services Ombudsman (Wales) Act 2005 (listed authorities), after the heading "Environment" insert— " The Committee on Climate Change. "

Schedule 2. Trading schemes

Section 46

Part 1. Schemes limiting activities

Introductory

1. This Part of this Schedule deals with trading schemes that operate by limiting or encouraging the limitation of activities that consist of the emission of greenhouse gas or that cause or contribute, directly or indirectly, to such emissions.

Trading periods

2. The regulations must specify the period or periods by reference to which the scheme is to operate (a "trading period").

Activities

3. (1)The regulations must identify the activities to which the trading scheme applies.
(2) The regulations may identify the activities by reference to any, or any combination of, criteria and in particular—
(a) may identify the activities by reference to the locations or locations at which they are carried on, or
(b) may be expressed to apply to all activities of a particular kind carried on in the United Kingdom or a part of the United Kingdom.
(3) The regulations must specify the units of measurement of the activities for the purposes of the scheme.
(4) The regulations may specify units of measurement by reference to—
(a) the activities themselves,
(b) anything consumed or used for the purposes of the activities,
(c) anything produced by the activities, or
(d) any other consequence of the activities.
(5) The regulations may, in particular, make provision—
(a) for activities to be measured by reference to the amount (in tonnes of carbon dioxide equivalent) of the greenhouse gas emissions for which those activities are to be regarded as responsible; and
(b) as to the method by which that amount is to be measured or calculated.
(6) The regulations may make different provision in relation to different descriptions of activity to which the scheme applies.

Participants

4. (1)The regulations must identify the persons to whom the trading scheme applies (the

"participants").

(2) The regulations—

(a) may identify the participants by reference to any, or any combination of, criteria, or

(b) provide for their identification by a specified person or body.

(3) The regulations may, in particular, identify or provide for the identification of the participants by reference to their responsibility for activities to which the trading scheme applies.

(4) The regulations may provide for more than one person to be treated as a single participant.

(5) The regulations may provide for persons to cease to be participants in circumstances specified in the regulations.

Allocation of allowances

5. (1)The regulations may provide for the allocation among the participants of allowances representing the right to carry on a specified amount of the activities in a trading period.

(2) The regulations may set a limit on—

(a) the total amount of the activities for a trading period, and

(b) the total amount of the allowances to be allocated for the period.

(3) The regulations may specify the method of allocation or provide for it to be determined in accordance with the regulations.

(4) The regulations may not provide for allowances to be allocated in return for consideration.

Use of allowances

6. (1)The regulations may require each participant to have or acquire enough allowances to match the participant's activities in a trading period, subject to any offsetting in accordance with provision made under paragraph 7.

(2) The regulations—

(a) may permit allowances held by a participant at the end of a trading period in excess of the participant's activities in the period to be used to cover the participant's activities in a later trading period,

(b) may permit allowances allocated to a participant for a trading period to be used to cover the participant's activities in an earlier trading period, and

(c) may in either case provide for such use of allowances to be subject to such conditions and limitations as may be specified in or determined in accordance with the regulations.

(3) The regulations must contain provision for ensuring that allowances used by a participant for the purposes of a trading scheme cannot be used by the participant for any other purpose.

(4) The regulations—

(a) may provide for the expiry of allowances after such period as may be specified in or determined in accordance with the regulations;

(b) may enable allowances to be cancelled by a person by whom they are held instead of being used for the purposes of a trading scheme.

Credits

7. (1)The regulations may enable participants to offset the carrying on of the activities in a trading period by acquiring credits representing—

(a) a reduction in an amount of greenhouse gas emissions, or

(b) the removal of an amount of greenhouse gas from the atmosphere.

(2) Regulations that make provision under this paragraph for a trading period must set a limit on the total amount of the activities for the period.

(3) If the regulations also provide for the allocation of allowances for the period, they must—

(a) set a limit on the total amount of the allowances to be allocated for the period, and

(b) require each participant to acquire enough credits to offset any activities carried on by the participant in the period in excess of those for which the participant has or has acquired allowances.

(4) Otherwise, such regulations must—

(a) set a limit on the amount of the activities that each participant may carry on in the period, and

(b) require each participant to acquire enough credits to offset any activities carried on by the participant in the period in excess of that limit.

(5) The regulations must specify—

(a) the descriptions of credits that may be used for offsetting a participant's activities,

(b) the value of different descriptions of credit as regards the amount of the activities they are treated as offsetting, and

(c) the circumstances in which credits of any description may be used for the purposes of the trading scheme.

(6) The regulations—

(a) must contain provision for ensuring that credits used to offset activities under a trading scheme cannot be used by the participant for any other purpose;

(b) may enable credits to be cancelled by a person by whom they are held instead of being used for that purpose.

Payments

8. (1)The regulations may provide that a participant who does not have or acquire enough allowances or credits to match or offset the participant's activities in a trading period must pay an amount specified in or determined in accordance with the regulations within the period so specified.

(2) The regulations may require the payment to be made to—

(a) the administrator, or

(b) such other person as the regulations may specify.

(3) The provision that may be made about the amount of the payment includes, in particular, provision—

(a) for the amount to be determined by the administrator or a national authority;

(b) in a case where the payment is not made within the period specified in the regulations, for the amount to increase at the rate so specified until payment;

(c) for the amount of the payment, or of any amount by reference to which it is to be calculated, to be adjusted from time to time by reference to inflation or some other factor.

(4) Provision within sub-paragraph (3)(c) may refer, in particular, to an index or data specified in the regulations (including as modified from time to time after the regulations come into force).

(5) If the regulations provide for payments to be made to a person other than a national authority, they must provide for that person to pay the sums received to the national authority or authorities specified in or determined in accordance with the regulations.

Trading

9. (1)The regulations must provide for the participants in a trading scheme to trade in any allowances or credits under the scheme.

(2) The regulations may also provide for trading in the allowances or credits by third parties authorised in accordance with the regulations.

(3) The regulations must specify the circumstances in which trading is permitted.

(4) The regulations may require trading to be notified to the administrator of the trading scheme.

Permits

10. (1)The regulations may provide that participants may only carry on activities to which the trading scheme applies, or specified activities to which the scheme applies, if they hold a permit.
(2) The regulations may make provision about the issue, variation, transfer, surrender and revocation of permits.
(3) The regulations may provide for conditions to be attached to permits.
(4) References in this Schedule to the requirements of the scheme include requirements imposed by conditions attached to a permit.

Units under other schemes

11. (1)The regulations may make provision for recognising any of the following as equivalent to allowances or credits under the trading scheme—
(a) allowances, credits or certificates under another trading scheme for which provision is made by regulations under this Part of this Act;
(b) units under any other trading scheme (at United Kingdom, European or international level) relating to greenhouse gas emissions.
(2) The regulations may provide—
(a) for determining the value for the purposes of the scheme of any such allowances, credits, certificates or units, and
(b) for the use for the purposes of the scheme of any such allowances, credits, certificates or units to be subject to such conditions and limitations as may be specified in or determined in accordance with the regulations.

Part 2. Schemes encouraging activities

Introductory

12. This Part of this Schedule deals with trading schemes that operate by encouraging activities that consist of, or that cause or contribute, directly or indirectly to—
(a) reductions in greenhouse gas emissions, or
(b) the removal of greenhouse gas from the atmosphere.

Trading periods

13. The regulations must specify the period or periods by reference to which the scheme is to operate (a "trading period").

Activities

14. (1)The regulations must identify the activities to which the trading scheme applies.
(2) The regulations may identify the activities by reference to any, or any combination of, criteria and in particular—
(a) may identify the activities by reference to the locations or locations at which they are carried on, or
(b) may be expressed to apply to all activities of a particular kind carried on in the United Kingdom or a part of the United Kingdom.
(3) The regulations must specify the units of measurement of the activities for the purposes of the

scheme.

(4) The regulations may specify units of measurement by reference to—

(a) the activities themselves,

(b) anything consumed or used for the purposes of the activities,

(c) anything produced by the activities, or

(d) any other consequence of the activities.

(5) The regulations may, in particular, make provision—

(a) for activities to be measured by reference to the amount (in tonnes of carbon dioxide equivalent) of the reduction of greenhouse gas emissions, or removals of greenhouse gas from the atmosphere, for which those activities are to be regarded as responsible; and

(b) as to the method by which that amount is to be measured or calculated.

(6) The regulations may make different provision in relation to different descriptions of activity to which the scheme applies.

Participants

15. (1)The regulations must identify the persons to whom the trading scheme applies (the "participants").

(2) The regulations—

(a) may identify the participants by reference to any, or any combination of, criteria, or

(b) provide for their identification by a specified person or body.

(3) The regulations may provide for more than one person to be treated as a single participant.

(4) The regulations may provide for persons to cease to be participants in circumstances specified in the regulations.

Targets and obligations

16. The regulations must, for each trading period—

(a) set a target for the total amount of the activities, and

(b) impose, or provide for the imposition of, an obligation on each participant in relation to the carrying on of a specified amount of the activities in the period.

Certificates

17. (1)The regulations must provide for the issue of certificates evidencing the carrying on of the activities in a trading period.

(2) The regulations may provide for certificates to evidence the carrying on of the activities—

(a) by the participant in question,

(b) by another participant in the trading scheme, or

(c) by a third party authorised in accordance with the regulations to obtain certificates for the purposes of the scheme.

(3) The regulations must require each participant to have enough certificates at the end of each trading period to comply with the participant's obligations under the trading scheme.

(4) The regulations must contain provision for ensuring that certificates used by a participant for that purpose cannot be used by the participant for any other purpose.

(5) The regulations—

(a) may provide for the expiry of certificates after such period as may be specified in or determined in accordance with the regulations;

(b) may enable certificates to be cancelled by a person by whom they are held instead of being used for the purposes of a trading scheme.

Payments

18. (1)The regulations may provide that a participant who does not have enough certificates at the end of a trading period to comply with the participant's obligations under the trading scheme must pay an amount specified in or determined in accordance with the regulations within the period so specified.
(2) The regulations may require the payment to be made to—
(a) the administrator, or
(b) such other person as the regulations may specify.
(3) The provision that may be made about the amount of the payment includes, in particular, provision—
(a) for the amount to be determined by the administrator or a national authority;
(b) in a case where the payment is not made within the period specified in the regulations, for the amount to increase at the rate so specified until payment;
(c) for the amount of the payment, or of any amount by reference to which it is to be calculated, to be adjusted from time to time by reference to inflation or some other factor.
(4) Provision within sub-paragraph (3)(c) may refer, in particular, to an index or data specified in the regulations (including as modified from time to time after the regulations come into force).
(5) If the regulations provide for payments to be made to a person other than a national authority, they must provide for that person to pay the sums received to the national authority or authorities specified in or determined in accordance with the regulations.

Trading

19. (1)The regulations must provide for the participants in a trading scheme to trade in certificates.
(2) The regulations may also provide for trading in certificates by third parties authorised in accordance with the regulations.
(3) The regulations must specify the circumstances in which trading is permitted.
(4) The regulations may require trading to be notified to the administrator of the trading scheme.

Units under other schemes

20. (1)The regulations may make provision for recognising any of the following as equivalent to certificates under the trading scheme—
(a) allowances, credits or certificates under another trading scheme for which provision is made by regulations under this Part of this Act;
(b) units under any other trading scheme (at United Kingdom, European or international level) relating to greenhouse gas emissions.
(2) The regulations may provide—
(a) for determining the value for the purposes of the scheme of any such allowances, credits, certificates or units, and
(b) for the use for the purposes of the scheme of any such allowances, credits, certificates or units to be subject to such conditions and limitations as may be specified in or determined in accordance with the regulations.

Part 3. Administration and enforcement

The administrator

21. (1)The regulations may appoint a person as the administrator of a trading scheme.

(2) The regulations may confer or impose functions on the administrator for the purposes of the scheme.

(3) Only the following may be appointed as the administrator of a trading scheme—

(a) the Secretary of State,

(b) the Scottish Ministers,

(c) the Welsh Ministers,

(d) the relevant Northern Ireland department,

(e) a body established by an enactment, or

(f) any combination of the above.

(4) The same person may be appointed as the administrator of more than one trading scheme.

(5) More than one person may be appointed as the administrator of the same trading scheme.

Information

22. (1)The regulations may require such information as may be specified in or determined in accordance with the regulations to be provided to—

(a) the administrator of a trading scheme,

(b) a national authority, or

(c) participants or potential participants in the scheme,

for purposes connected with the scheme.

(2) The regulations may confer power on the administrator of a trading scheme to require information to be provided to any of those persons for those purposes.

(3) The regulations must provide for a requirement by the administrator to provide information to be notified in writing to the person to whom it is made.

(4) If the regulations confer functions on the administrator for the purposes of this paragraph, they may provide for the administrator to delegate the performance of any of those functions.

(5) The regulations may provide for information held by or on behalf of the administrator of a trading scheme in connection with the administrator's functions to be disclosed to—

(a) any other administrator of the scheme,

(b) the administrator of another trading scheme, or

(c) a national authority.

Registers

23. (1)The regulations may provide for the creation and maintenance of a register or registers of information relating to a trading scheme and, in particular, for the register or registers to keep track of any of the following—

(a) the participants in a trading scheme;

(b) any limits on or obligations applying to the participants' activities under the scheme;

(c) any allocation of allowances among the participants;

(d) the allowances, credits, certificates or other units held by the participants or others;

(e) trading in allowances, credits, certificates or other units;

(f) the use by the participants or others of allowances, credits, certificates or other units for the purposes of the scheme;

(g) the cancellation of allowances, credits, certificates or other units;

(h) permits held by the participants, and any conditions attached to those permits.

(2) The regulations may, in particular, provide for the establishment and maintenance of accounts in which allowances, credits, certificates or other units may be held by the participants, the administrator or others and between which they may be transferred.

(3) The regulations may provide for the same register to operate in relation to more than one trading scheme.

(4) The regulations may make provision for the disclosure of information held in or derived from a

register relating to a trading scheme—

(a) for the purposes of the administration of another trading scheme for which provision is made by regulations under this Part of this Act, or

(b) for the purposes of the administration of any other trading scheme (at United Kingdom, European or international level) relating to greenhouse gas emissions.

Publication of information

24. The regulations may confer or impose functions on the administrator of a trading scheme in relation to the publication of information relating to the scheme or its participants (including, in particular, information supplied to the administrator by the participants and others).

Acquisition of units by the administrator

25. The regulations may confer powers on the administrator of a trading scheme to acquire—

(a) allowances, credits or certificates under another trading scheme for which provision is made by regulations under this Part of this Act, or

(b) units under any other trading scheme (at United Kingdom, European or international level) relating to greenhouse gas emissions.

Charges

26. (1)The regulations may—

(a) require the payment by participants or other persons authorised to trade in allowances, credits or certificates of charges of an amount determined by or under the regulations by reference to the costs of operating the scheme, and

(b) provide for such charges to be imposed by—

(i) a national authority,

(ii) the administrator of the scheme, or

(iii) such other person as may be specified in or determined in accordance with the regulations.

(2) If the regulations provide for charges to be payable to a person other than a national authority, they must provide for that person to pay the sums received to the national authority or authorities specified in or determined in accordance with the regulations.

Monitoring compliance

27. (1)The regulations may make provision for monitoring compliance with the requirements of a trading scheme.

(2) The regulations may, in particular, make provision about—

(a) the keeping of records by the participants,

(b) the provision of information by the participants and others,

(c) the audit and verification of that information, and

(d) the inspection of premises.

(3) If the regulations confer functions on the administrator of the scheme for the purposes of this paragraph, they may provide for the administrator to delegate the performance of any of those functions.

Enforcement

28. (1)The regulations may confer powers on a person to whom this paragraph applies to—

(a) require the production of documents or the provision of information,

(b) question the officers of a company,

(c) enter premises with a warrant, or

(d) seize documents or records.

(2) The regulations must provide that the power in question may only be exercised where the person on whom it is conferred reasonably believes there has been a failure to comply with the requirements of a trading scheme.

(3) This paragraph applies to—

(a) a national authority,

(b) the administrator of the scheme, and

(c) such other person as may be specified in or determined in accordance with the regulations.

Penalties

29. (1)The regulations may provide that a person is liable to a financial or other penalty if the person fails to comply with the requirements of a trading scheme.

(2) The regulations may—

(a) specify the amount of any financial penalty, or

(b) provide for the amount of any financial penalty to be determined in accordance with the regulations.

(3) If the regulations provide for financial penalties to be payable to a person other than a national authority, they must provide for that person to pay the sums received to the national authority or authorities specified in or determined in accordance with the regulations.

Offences

30. (1)The regulations may create offences relating to trading schemes.

(2) The regulations may provide for such an offence to be triable—

(a) only summarily, or

(b) either summarily or on indictment.

(3) The regulations may provide for such an offence to be punishable on summary conviction—

(a) with imprisonment for a term not exceeding such period as is specified in the regulations (which may not exceed the normal maximum term),

(b) with a fine not exceeding such amount as is so specified (which may not exceed £50,000), or

(c) with both.

(4) The "normal maximum term" means—

(a) in relation to England and Wales—

(i) in the case of an offence triable only summarily, 51 weeks, and

(ii) in the case of an offence triable either summarily or on indictment, twelve months;

(b) in relation to Scotland—

(i) in the case of an offence triable only summarily, 6 months, and

(ii) in the case of an offence triable either summarily or on indictment, twelve months;

(c) in relation to Northern Ireland, six months.

(5) Regulations that—

(a) are made before the date on which section 281. (5) of the Criminal Justice Act 2003 (c. 44) comes into force, and

(b) in relation to England and Wales, make provision for a summary offence to be punishable with a term of imprisonment exceeding six months,

must provide that, where the offence is committed before that date, it is punishable with imprisonment for a term not exceeding six months.

(6) Regulations that—

(a) are made before the date on which section 154. (1) of the Criminal Justice Act 2003 comes into force, and

(b) in relation to England and Wales, make provision for an offence triable either summarily or on indictment to be punishable on summary conviction with a term of imprisonment exceeding six months,

must provide that, where the offence is committed before that date, it is punishable on summary conviction with imprisonment for a term not exceeding six months.

(7) The regulations may provide for an offence to be punishable on indictment—

(a) with imprisonment for a term not exceeding such period as is specified in the regulations (which may not exceed five years),

(b) with a fine, or

(c) with both.

(8) The regulations may—

(a) provide for defences against offences, and

(b) make provision about matters of procedure and evidence in proceedings relating to offences.

Appeals

31. (1)The regulations may confer rights of appeal against—

(a) decisions made in relation to a trading scheme, and

(b) civil penalties imposed or enforcement action taken for failure to comply with the requirements of a trading scheme.

(2) The regulations must specify the court, tribunal or person who is to hear and determine appeals in relation to a trading scheme.

(3) The regulations may, in particular, provide for appeals in relation to a trading scheme to be heard by—

(a) a national authority, if not the administrator of the trading scheme, or

(b) a person appointed by a national authority for that purpose.

(4) They may provide for an appeal to be determined by a person other than the person by whom the appeal was heard.

Schedule 3. Trading schemes regulations: further provisions

Section 49

Part 1. Regulations made by a single national authority

1. This Part of this Schedule applies in relation to an instrument containing regulations under this Part of this Act made by a single national authority.

2. (1)Where the instrument contains regulations that—

(a) are to be made by the Secretary of State, and

(b) are subject to affirmative resolution procedure,

the regulations must not be made unless a draft of the statutory instrument containing them has been laid before and approved by a resolution of each House of Parliament.

(2) Where the instrument contains regulations that—

(a) are to be made by a national authority other than the Secretary of State, and

(b) are subject to affirmative resolution procedure,

the regulations must not be made unless a draft of the statutory instrument containing them has been laid before and approved by a resolution of the relevant devolved legislature.

3. (1)An instrument containing regulations made by the Secretary of State that are subject to

negative resolution procedure is subject to annulment in pursuance of a resolution of either House of Parliament.

(2) An instrument containing regulations made by the Scottish Ministers that are subject to negative resolution procedure is subject to annulment in pursuance of a resolution of the Scottish Parliament.

(3) An instrument containing regulations made by the Welsh Ministers that are subject to negative resolution procedure is subject to annulment in pursuance of a resolution of the National Assembly for Wales.

(4) An instrument containing regulations made by a Northern Ireland department that are subject to negative resolution procedure is subject to negative resolution within the meaning of section 41.

(6) of the Interpretation Act (Northern Ireland) 1954 (c. 33 (N.I.)) as if it were a statutory instrument within the meaning of that Act.

4. Any provision that may be made by regulations subject to negative resolution procedure may be made by regulations subject to affirmative resolution procedure.

Part 2. Regulations made by two or more national authorities

5. This Part of this Schedule applies in relation to an instrument containing regulations under this Part of this Act made or to be made by any two or more of—

(a) the Secretary of State,

(b) the Welsh Ministers, and

(c) a Northern Ireland department.

6. If any of the regulations are subject to affirmative resolution procedure, all of them are subject to that procedure.

7. Paragraphs 2 and 3 (affirmative and negative resolution procedure) apply to the instrument as they apply to an instrument containing regulations made by a single national authority.

8. (1)If in accordance with paragraph 3 (negative resolution procedure)—

(a) either House of Parliament resolves that an address be presented to Her Majesty praying that an instrument containing regulations made by the Secretary of State be annulled, or

(b) a devolved legislature resolves that an instrument containing regulations made by a national authority be annulled,

nothing further is to be done under the instrument after the date of the resolution and Her Majesty may by Order in Council revoke the instrument.

(2) This is without prejudice to the validity of anything previously done under the instrument or to the making of a new instrument.

(3) This paragraph applies in place of provision made by any other enactment about the effect of such a resolution.

Part 3. Power to make provision by Order in Council

9. (1)Her Majesty may by Order in Council make provision for trading schemes.

(2) That power may only be exercised to make an Order in Council—

(a) that extends or applies both to Scotland and to one or more of England, Wales and Northern Ireland, or

(b) that extends to Scotland only and contains both provision within the legislative competence of the Scottish Parliament and provision outside that competence.

(3) The provision that may be made by an Order in Council under this paragraph includes any provision that may be made by a national authority by regulations under this Part of this Act.

10. No recommendation is to be made to Her Majesty in Council to make an Order in Council under paragraph 9 unless the requirements of section 48. (1) and (2) as to advice and consultation have been complied with.

11. (1)This paragraph applies to an Order in Council under paragraph 9 containing any provision

that, were it to be made by regulations under this Part of this Act, would be subject to affirmative resolution procedure.

(2) No recommendation is to be made to Her Majesty in Council to make an Order in Council to which this paragraph applies unless—

(a) in the case of an Order in Council containing provision that may be made by the Secretary of State by regulations under this Part of this Act, a draft of the statutory instrument containing the Order in Council has been laid before, and approved by a resolution of, each House of Parliament, and

(b) in the case of an Order in Council containing provision that may be made by a national authority other than the Secretary of State by regulations under this Part of this Act, a draft of the statutory instrument containing the Order in Council has been laid before, and approved by a resolution of, the relevant devolved legislature.

12. (1)This paragraph applies to an Order in Council under paragraph 9 other than one to which paragraph 11 applies.

(2) An Order in Council to which this paragraph applies containing provision that may be made by the Secretary of State by regulations under this Part of this Act is subject to annulment in pursuance of a resolution of either House of Parliament.

(3) An Order in Council to which this paragraph applies containing provision that may be made by the Scottish Ministers by regulations under this Part of this Act is subject to annulment in pursuance of a resolution of the Scottish Parliament.

(4) An Order in Council to which this paragraph applies containing provision that may be made by the Welsh Ministers by regulations under this Part of this Act is subject to annulment in pursuance of a resolution of the National Assembly for Wales.

(5) An Order in Council to which this paragraph applies containing provision that may be made by a Northern Ireland department by regulations under this Part of this Act is subject to negative resolution within the meaning of section 41. (6) of the Interpretation Act (Northern Ireland) 1954 (c. 33 (N.I.)) as if it were a statutory instrument within the meaning of that Act.

13. (1)If in accordance with paragraph 12—

(a) either House of Parliament resolves that an address be presented to Her Majesty praying that an Order in Council be annulled, or

(b) a devolved legislature resolves that an Order in Council be annulled,

nothing further is to be done under the Order in Council after the date of the resolution and Her Majesty may by Order in Council revoke it.

(2) This is without prejudice to the validity of anything previously done under the Order in Council or to the making of a new Order in Council.

(3) This paragraph applies in place of provision made by any other enactment about the effect of such a resolution.

Schedule 4. Trading schemes: powers to require information

Section 50

Introductory

1[F1. (1)The powers conferred by this Schedule are exercisable by the following authorities—

(a) the Secretary of State;

(b) the Scottish Ministers;

(c) the relevant Northern Ireland department;

(d) the Welsh Ministers;

(e) the Environment Agency;

(f) the Scottish Environment Protection Agency.

(2) References in this Schedule to an "environmental authority" are to any of those authorities.]

Amendments (Textual)

F1. Sch. 4 paras. 1-5 ceased to have effect (26.1.2009) by virtue of Climate Change Act 2008 (c. 27), ss. 50. (2), 100. (5)

Information from electricity suppliers and distributors

2[F1. (1)An environmental authority may, for the purposes of enabling a trading scheme to be established, by notice require an electricity supplier or electricity distributor to provide any of the following information—

(a) information about the electricity meters and metering systems for which the supplier or distributor is responsible, including (in particular) their locations and any identifying features;

(b) information about the persons to whom electricity measured by those meters or systems is supplied or who purchase such electricity;

(c) information about the consumption by those persons of that electricity;

(d) any other information that the environmental authority considers necessary for identifying the potential participants in the scheme.

(2) An "electricity supplier"—

(a) in relation to England and Wales and Scotland means an authorised supplier within the meaning of the Electricity Act 1989 (c. 29) (see section 64. (1) of that Act);

(b) in relation to Northern Ireland means—

(i) an electricity supplier within the meaning of the Electricity (Northern Ireland) Order 1992 (S.I. 1992/231) (N.I. 1) (see Article 3 of that Order), or

(ii) a person who may supply electricity to premises without a licence by virtue of an exemption under Article 9 of that Order.

(3) An "electricity distributor"—

(a) in relation to England and Wales and Scotland means an authorised distributor within the meaning of the Electricity Act 1989 (see section 64. (1) of that Act);

(b) in relation to Northern Ireland means an electricity distributor within the meaning of the Electricity (Northern Ireland) Order 1992 (see Article 3 of that Order).

(4) References in this Schedule to an electricity supplier or electricity distributor include an agent of such a supplier or distributor.]

Information from potential participants in a trading scheme

3[F1. (1)An environmental authority may, for the purposes of enabling a trading scheme to be established, by notice require a potential participant in the scheme to provide any of the following information—

(a) information about whether the criteria specified in the notice are met by the potential participant, either alone or together with any other person or persons;

(b) information identifying any potential co-participant;

(c) contact details for the potential participant and any potential co-participant;

(d) information about the meters that measure electricity supplied to or purchased by the potential participant or any potential co-participant;

(e) information about the consumption of electricity by the potential participant and any potential co-participant;

(f) information about any climate change agreement (within the meaning of Schedule 6 to the Finance Act 2000 (c. 17)) entered into by or on behalf of the potential participant or any potential co-participant.

(2) A "potential participant", in relation to a trading scheme, means a person who the

environmental authority considers—

(a) will or may be a participant in the scheme, or

(b) will or may fall to be treated together with any other person or persons (a "potential co-participant") as such a participant.]

Requirements for a valid notice

4[F1. (1)A notice under this Schedule must comply with the following requirements.

(2) The notice must—

(a) be in writing,

(b) specify the information to be provided,

(c) specify the name and address of the person to whom the information is to be provided,

(d) specify the date by which the information is to be provided, and

(e) explain the consequences of failure to comply with the notice.

(3) An environmental authority must not give a notice requiring information from a person unless—

(a) the authority has previously sent the person a request in writing for the information, and

(b) the person has failed to provide the information within the period of 28 days beginning with the day on which the request was sent.]

Failure to comply with notice etc an offence

5[F1. (1)A person who—

(a) fails without reasonable excuse to comply with a notice under this Schedule, or

(b) provides information in response to such a notice that the person knows or suspects to be false or misleading, commits an offence.

(2) A person guilty of such an offence is liable on summary conviction to a fine not exceeding level 5 on the standard scale.]

Disclosure of information

6. (1)This paragraph applies to information obtained by an environmental authority (whether or not pursuant to a notice under this Schedule) from—

(a) an electricity supplier or electricity distributor, or

(b) a potential participant,

for the purposes of enabling a trading scheme to be established.

(2) The information may be disclosed for the purposes of or in connection with the establishment, operation or enforcement of a trading scheme—

(a) by an environmental authority to another environmental authority or the administrator of the scheme, or

(b) by the administrator of the scheme to any other administrator of the scheme or an environmental authority.

(3) This does not affect any other right to disclose information within sub-paragraph (1) apart from this paragraph.

Schedule 5. Waste reduction schemes

Section 71

. . . .

Amendments (Textual)

F1. Sch. 5 repealed (15.1.2012) by Localism Act 2011 (c. 20), ss. 47. (a), 240. (1)(e), Sch. 25 Pts. 8

Schedule 6. Charges for carrier bags

Section 77
Amendments (Textual)
F1. Words in Sch. 6 para. 2 substituted (N.I.) (28.4.2014) by Carrier Bags Act (Northern Ireland) 2014 (c. 7), s. 1. (b)

Part 1. +N.I.Powers to make regulations about charges

General power+N.I.

1. The relevant national authority may make provision by regulations about charging by sellers of goods for the supply of [F1single use carrier bags][F1carrier bags].+N.I.

Requirement to charge+N.I.

2. The regulations may make provision requiring sellers of goods to charge for [F1single use carrier bags][F1carrier bags] supplied—+N.I.
[F2. (a)at a place where goods are sold, for the purpose of enabling goods to be taken away, or]
[F2at the place where the goods are sold, for the purpose of enabling the goods to be taken away, or]
[F2. (b)for the purpose of enabling goods to be delivered.]
[F2for the purpose of enabling the goods to be delivered.]
Amendments (Textual)
F2. Sch. 6 para. 2. (a)(b) substituted (N.I.) (28.4.2014) by Carrier Bags Act (Northern Ireland) 2014 (c. 7), s. 3. (1)
[F32. AThe regulations may make provision for treating carrier bags as having been supplied for the purpose of enabling goods to be taken away if the carrier bags have been designed for that purpose.]+N.I.
Amendments (Textual)
F3. Sch. 6 para. 2. A inserted (N.I.) (28.4.2014) by Carrier Bags Act (Northern Ireland) 2014 (c. 7), s. 3. (2)

Sellers of goods+N.I.

3. (1)"Seller", in relation to goods, has the meaning given by the regulations which may define that term by reference (in particular) to—+N.I.
(a) a person's involvement in selling the goods,
(b) a person's interest in the goods, or
(c) a person's interest in the place at or from which the goods are sold,
or any combination of those factors.
(2) The regulations may make provision for regulations under this Schedule to apply—
(a) to all sellers of goods,
(b) to sellers of goods named in the regulations,
(c) to sellers of goods identified by reference to specified factors, or

(d) to sellers of goods within paragraph (b) and sellers of goods within paragraph (c).

(3) The specified factors may include—

(a) the place or places at or from which a seller supplies goods;

(b) the type of goods that a seller supplies;

(c) the value of goods that a seller supplies;

(d) a seller's turnover or any part of that turnover.

[F4. (e)the number of a seller's full-time equivalent employees.]

(4) In this Schedule "specified" means specified in regulations under this Schedule.

[F5. (5)For the purposes of sub-paragraph (3)(e), the number of a seller's full-time equivalent employees is calculated as follows—

Step 1 Find the number for full-time employees of the seller.

Step 2 Add, for each employee of the seller who is not a full-time employee, such fraction as is just and reasonable. The result is the number of full-time equivalent employees.]

Amendments (Textual)

F4. Sch. 6 para. 3. (5) inserted (N.I.) (28.4.2014) by Carrier Bags Act (Northern Ireland) 2014 (c. 7), s. 4. (3)

F5. Sch. 6 para. 3. (3)(e) inserted (N.I.) (28.4.2014) by Carrier Bags Act (Northern Ireland) 2014 (c. 7), s. 4. (2)

Amount of charge+N.I.

4. The regulations may specify the minimum amount that a seller must charge for each [F6single use carrier bag][F6carrier bag], or provide for that amount to be determined in accordance with the regulations.+N.I.

Amendments (Textual)

F6 Words in Act substituted (N.I.) (28.4.2014) by Carrier Bags Act (Northern Ireland) 2014 (c. 7) , s. 1. (a)

Destination of proceeds – Wales+N.I.

[F74. A(1)This paragraph applies to regulations made by the Welsh Ministers in relation to Wales.

(2) The regulations may provide for the application of the net proceeds of the charge to specified purposes.

[F8. (2. A)The regulations may—

(a) provide for the time when and manner in which the gross or net proceeds of the charge are to be paid to the Department;

(b) provide for the payment of interest for late payment of the gross or net proceeds of the charge to the Department.]

(3) Regulations under sub-paragraph (2) may (among other things)–

(a) require sellers to apply the net proceeds of the charge to any one or more specified purposes;

(b) provide for any duty imposed under paragraph (a) to be discharged (subject to any provision made under paragraph (c)) by the net proceeds of the charge being accepted by any one or more of the following persons–

(i) specified persons;

(ii) persons who fall within a specified category of person;

(c) make provision about the arrangements under which the net proceeds of the charge are to be given by sellers to the persons mentioned in paragraph (b) or any other person;

(d) require persons who accept any net proceeds of the charge under paragraph (b) to apply the proceeds to any one or more specified purposes;

(e) provide for recovery by the Welsh Ministers of sums equal to the proceeds of the charge that have been accepted or applied otherwise than in accordance with provision made under sub-paragraph (2);

(f) provide for the application of sums recovered under paragraph (e) to specified purposes (this includes making provision to the effect that such sums are not to be paid into the Welsh Consolidated Fund);

(g) require the Welsh Ministers to give guidance about compliance with the regulations.

(4) The purposes that may be specified under sub-paragraph (2) are limited to purposes relating to any of the following–

(a) preventing or reducing waste;

(b) the collection, management, treatment or disposal of waste;

(c) protecting or improving the environment in relation to pollution or nuisances;

(d) educational or recreational activities for children or young people which relate to any of the matters specified in paragraphs (a) to (c).

(5) But purposes concerning the production of renewable energy for consumption in transport or the use of that energy in transport may not be specified under sub-paragraph (2).

(6) The regulations may make provision for regulations under this Schedule to apply to persons other than sellers, if the Welsh Ministers consider that such provision is appropriate for the enforcement of provision made under sub-paragraph (2) or for otherwise making such provision effective.

(7) The specified factors under paragraph 3. (2)(c) may also include–

(a) a seller's arrangements for applying the net proceeds of the charge, or

(b) any other factor that the Welsh Ministers consider appropriate, whether or not that factor is of the same kind as the factors listed in that paragraph.

(8) The regulations may provide for exceptions and exemptions.]

Amendments (Textual)

F7. Sch. 6 paras. 4. A, 4. B inserted (E.W.) (15.2.2011) by Waste (Wales) Measure 2010 (nawm 8), ss. 1. (2), 21. (2)

F8. Sch. 6 para. 4. A(2. A) inserted (N.I.) (28.4.2014) by Carrier Bags Act (Northern Ireland) 2014 (c. 7), s. 5

[F94. A(1)This paragraph applies to regulations made by the Department in relation to Northern Ireland.+N.I.

(2) The regulations may require the seller to pay to the Department—

(a) the gross proceeds of the charge, or

(b) the net proceeds of the charge.

(3) Paragraph 7. (3)(c) does not apply to any amount required by regulations made under this paragraph to be paid to the Department.

(4) In this paragraph—

" the Department " means the Department of the Environment in Northern Ireland;

" gross proceeds of the charge " means the amount received by the seller by way of charges for [F1 single use carrier bags] [F1 carrier bags] ;

" net proceeds of the charge " means the seller's gross proceeds of the charge reduced by such amounts as may be specified.]

Amendments (Textual)

F9. Sch. 6 para. 4. A inserted (N.I.) (4.5.2011) by Single Use Carrier Bags Act (Northern Ireland) 2011 (c. 26), s. 1. (1)

Interpretation of paragraph 4. A+N.I.

[F74. B(1)This paragraph applies for the purposes of paragraph 4. A.

(2) " Children " means persons who have not attained the age of 18.

(3) " Pollution " means pollution of the air, water or land which may give rise to any environmental harm, including (but not limited to) pollution caused by light, noise, heat or vibrations or any other kind of release of energy.

(4) For the purposes of the definition in sub-paragraph (3), " environmental harm " means any of

the following–

(a) harm to the health of humans and other living organisms;

(b) harm to the quality of the environment, including–

(i) harm to the quality of the environment taken as a whole,

(ii) harm to the quality of the air, water or land, and

(iii) other impairment of, or interference with, the ecological systems of which any living organisms form part;

(c) offence to the senses of human beings;

(d) damage to property;

(e) impairment of, or interference with, the amenity of the environment or any legitimate use of the environment.

(5) For the purposes of sub-paragraphs (3) and (4), " air " includes (but is not limited to) air within buildings and air within other natural or man-made structures above or below ground.

(6) " Nuisance " means an act or omission affecting any place, or a state of affairs in any place, which may impair, or interfere with, the amenity of the environment or any legitimate use of the environment.

(7) " Net proceeds of the charge " has the same meaning as in paragraph 7. (4).

(8) " Young people " means persons who have attained the age of 18, but not the age of 25.]

Amendments (Textual)

F7. Sch. 6 paras. 4. A, 4. B inserted (E.W.) (15.2.2011) by Waste (Wales) Measure 2010 (nawm 8), ss. 1. (2), 21. (2)

[F1. Single use carrier bags][F1. Carrier bags]+N.I.

5[F10. (1)]"[F6. Single use carrier bag][F6. Carrier bag]" has the meaning given by the regulations, which may define that term by reference (in particular) to—+N.I.

(a) a bag's size, thickness, construction, composition or other characteristics, [F11or]

(b) its intended use, [F12or

(c) its price,]

or any combination of those factors.

[F13. (2) In this paragraph " price " means the price paid by a specified person, excluding any minimum charge that may be applicable by virtue of paragraph 4.]

Amendments (Textual)

F10 Sch. 6 para. 5 renumbered as Sch. 6 para. 5. (1) (N.I.) (28.4.2014) by Carrier Bags Act (Northern Ireland) 2014 (c. 7) , s. 6. (2)

F11 Word in Sch. 6 para. 5. (1)(a) omitted (N.I.) (28.4.2014) by virtue of Carrier Bags Act (Northern Ireland) 2014 (c. 7) , s. 6. (3)(a)

F12 Sch. 6 para. 5. (1)(c) and preceding word inserted (N.I.) (28.4.2014) by Carrier Bags Act (Northern Ireland) 2014 (c. 7) , s. 6. (3)(b)

F13 Sch. 6 para. 5. (2) inserted (N.I.) (28.4.2014) by Carrier Bags Act (Northern Ireland) 2014 (c. 7) , s. 6. (4)

Administration+N.I.

6. (1)The regulations may appoint a person (an "administrator") to administer provision made by regulations under this Schedule.+N.I.

(2) More than one person may be appointed as administrator.

(3) The regulations may confer or impose powers or duties on an administrator and may (in particular) do so—

(a) by making modifications to any enactment applying to the administrator, or

(b) by providing for any such enactment to apply, with or without modifications, for the purposes of regulations under this Schedule.

(4) References in this Schedule to an administrator include a person appointed by an administrator.

Record-keeping and publication of records+N.I.

7. (1)The regulations may require records to be kept relating to charges made for [F1single use carrier bags][F1carrier bags].+N.I.

(2) The regulations may require—

(a) the records, or such other information as may be specified, to be published at such times and in such manner as may be specified;

(b) the records, or such other information as may be specified, to be supplied on request and in such manner as may be specified to—

(i) the relevant national authority,

(ii) an administrator, or

(iii) members of the public.

(3) The regulations may (in particular) require the publication or supply of records or information relating to any of the following—

(a) the amount received by a seller by way of charges for [F1single use carrier bags][F1carrier bags];

(b) the seller's gross or net proceeds of the charge;

(c) the uses to which the net proceeds of the charge have been put.

[F14. (d)payments of the gross or net proceeds of the charge made to the Department of the Environment in Northern Ireland.]

[F15. (3. A)Regulations made by the Welsh Ministers may also require the publication or supply of records or information relating to the amount received by a person from a seller by way of net proceeds of the charge to be applied to purposes specified under paragraph 4. A(2).]

(4) In this paragraph—

"gross proceeds of the charge" means the amount received by the seller by way of charges for [F1single use carrier bags][F1carrier bags];

"net proceeds of the charge" means the seller's gross proceeds of the charge reduced by such amounts as may be specified.

Amendments (Textual)

F14. Sch. 6 para. 7. (3)(d) inserted (N.I.) (28.4.2014) by Carrier Bags Act (Northern Ireland) 2014 (c. 7), s. 7. (2)

F15. Sch. 6 para. 7. (3. A) inserted (E.W.) (15.2.2011) by Waste (Wales) Measure 2010 (nawm 8), ss. 1. (3), 21. (2)

Enforcement+N.I.

8. (1)The regulations may confer or impose powers or duties on an administrator to enforce provision made by regulations under this Schedule.+N.I.

(2) The regulations may (in particular) confer powers on an administrator to—

(a) require the production of documents or the provision of information,[F16 or]

[F17. (aa)inspect, retain or copy such documents, or]

(b) question a seller or officers or employees of a seller.

[F18. (2. A)Regulations made by the Welsh Ministers may also confer powers on an administrator to question a person the administrator reasonably believes has received any net proceeds of the charge or officers or employees of such a person.]

[F19. (3)Regulations under sub-paragraph (2) must contain provision for ensuring that the power in question is exercised by a person only where the person reasonably believes there has been a failure to comply with a requirement of regulations under this Schedule.]

Amendments (Textual)

F16. Word in Sch. 6 para. 8. (2)(a) omitted (N.I.) (28.4.2014) by virtue of Carrier Bags Act

(Northern Ireland) 2014 (c. 7), s. 7. (3)(a)

F17. Sch. 6 para. 8. (2)(aa) inserted (N.I.) (28.4.2014) by Carrier Bags Act (Northern Ireland) 2014 (c. 7), s. 7. (3)(b)

F18. Sch. 6 para. 8. (2. A) inserted (E.W.) (15.2.2011) by Waste (Wales) Measure 2010 (nawm 8), ss. 1. (4), 21. (2)

F19. Sch. 6 para. 8. (3) omitted (N.I.) (28.4.2014) by virtue of Carrier Bags Act (Northern Ireland) 2014 (c. 7), s. 7. (3)(c)

Part 2. +N.I.Civil sanctions

Civil sanctions+N.I.

9. (1)The relevant national authority may make provision by regulations about civil sanctions for breaches of regulations under this Schedule.+N.I.

(2) For the purposes of this Schedule a person breaches regulations under this Schedule if, in such circumstances as may be specified, the person—

(a) fails to comply with a requirement made by or under the regulations, or

(b) obstructs or fails to assist an administrator.

(3) In this Schedule "civil sanction" means—

(a) a fixed monetary penalty (see paragraph 10), or

(b) a discretionary requirement (see paragraph 12).

Fixed monetary penalties+N.I.

10. (1)The regulations may make provision conferring on an administrator the power by notice to impose a fixed monetary penalty on a person who breaches regulations under this Schedule.+N.I.

(2) The regulations may only confer such a power in relation to a case where the administrator is satisfied on the balance of probabilities that the breach has occurred.

(3) For the purposes of this Schedule a "fixed monetary penalty" is a requirement to pay to an administrator a penalty of an amount specified in or determined in accordance with the regulations.

(4) The regulations may not provide for the imposition of a fixed monetary penalty in excess of £5,000.

Fixed monetary penalties: procedure+N.I.

11. (1)Provision under paragraph 10 must secure that—+N.I.

(a) where an administrator proposes to impose a fixed monetary penalty on a person, the administrator must serve on that person a notice of what is proposed (a "notice of intent") that complies with sub-paragraph (2),

(b) the notice of intent also offers the person the opportunity to discharge the person's liability for the fixed monetary penalty by payment of a specified sum (which must be less than or equal to the amount of the penalty),

(c) if the person does not so discharge liability—

(i) the person may make written representations and objections to the administrator in relation to the proposed imposition of the fixed monetary penalty, and

(ii) the administrator must at the end of the period for making representations and objections decide whether to impose the fixed monetary penalty,

(d) where the administrator decides to impose the fixed monetary penalty, the notice imposing it ("the final notice") complies with sub-paragraph (4), and

(e) the person on whom a fixed monetary penalty is imposed may appeal against the decision to impose it.

(2) To comply with this sub-paragraph the notice of intent must include information as to—

(a) the grounds for the proposal to impose the fixed monetary penalty,

(b) the effect of payment of the sum referred to in sub-paragraph (1)(b),

(c) the right to make representations and objections,

(d) the circumstances in which the administrator may not impose the fixed monetary penalty,

(e) the period within which liability to the fixed monetary penalty may be discharged, which may not exceed the period of 28 days beginning with the day on which the notice of intent was received, and

(f) the period within which representations and objections may be made, which may not exceed the period of 28 days beginning with the day on which the notice of intent was received.

(3) Provision pursuant to sub-paragraph (1)(c)(ii) must include provision for circumstances in which the administrator may not decide to impose a fixed monetary penalty.

(4) To comply with this sub-paragraph the final notice referred to in sub-paragraph (1)(d) must include information as to—

(a) the grounds for imposing the penalty,

(b) how payment may be made,

(c) the period within which payment must be made,

(d) any early payment discounts or late payment penalties,

(e) rights of appeal, and

(f) the consequences of non-payment.

(5) Provision pursuant to sub-paragraph (1)(e) must secure that the grounds on which a person may appeal against a decision of the administrator include the following—

(a) that the decision was based on an error of fact;

(b) that the decision was wrong in law;

(c) that the decision was unreasonable.

Discretionary requirements+N.I.

12. (1)The regulations may make provision conferring on an administrator the power by notice to impose one or more discretionary requirements on a person who breaches regulations under this Schedule.+N.I.

(2) The regulations may only confer such a power in relation to a case where the administrator is satisfied on the balance of probabilities that the breach has occurred.

(3) For the purposes of this Schedule a "discretionary requirement" means—

(a) a requirement to pay a monetary penalty to an administrator of such amount as the administrator may determine, or

(b) a requirement to take such steps as an administrator may specify, within such period as the administrator may specify, to secure that the breach does not continue or recur.

(4) In this Schedule—

"variable monetary penalty" means a requirement referred to in sub-paragraph (3)(a);

"non-monetary discretionary requirement" means a requirement referred to in sub-paragraph (3)(b).

(5) The regulations must, in relation to each kind of breach of regulations under this Schedule for which a variable monetary penalty may be imposed—

(a) specify the maximum penalty that may be imposed for a breach of that kind, or

(b) provide for that maximum to be determined in accordance with the regulations.

(6) The regulations may not permit discretionary requirements to be imposed on a person on more than one occasion in relation to the same act or omission.

Discretionary requirements: procedure+N.I.

13. (1)Provision under paragraph 12 must secure that—+N.I.

(a) where an administrator proposes to impose a discretionary requirement on a person, the administrator must serve on that person a notice of what is proposed (a "notice of intent") that complies with sub-paragraph (2),

(b) that person may make written representations and objections to the administrator in relation to the proposed imposition of the discretionary requirement,

(c) after the end of the period for making such representations and objections, the administrator must decide whether to—

(i) impose the discretionary requirement, with or without modifications, or

(ii) impose any other discretionary requirement that the administrator has power to impose under paragraph 12,

(d) where the administrator decides to impose a discretionary requirement, the notice imposing it (the "final notice") complies with sub-paragraph (4), and

(e) the person on whom a discretionary requirement is imposed may appeal against the decision to impose it.

(2) To comply with this sub-paragraph the notice of intent must include information as to—

(a) the grounds for the proposal to impose the discretionary requirement,

(b) the right to make representations and objections,

(c) the circumstances in which the administrator may not impose the discretionary requirement,

(d) the period within which representations and objections may be made, which may not be less than the period of 28 days beginning with the day on which the notice of intent is received.

(3) Provision pursuant to sub-paragraph (1)(c) must include provision for circumstances in which the administrator may not decide to impose a fixed monetary penalty.

(4) To comply with this sub-paragraph the final notice referred to in sub-paragraph (1)(d) must include information as to—

(a) the grounds for imposing the discretionary requirement,

(b) where the discretionary requirement is a variable monetary penalty—

(i) how payment may be made,

(ii) the period within which payment must be made, and

(iii) any early payment discounts or late payment penalties,

(c) rights of appeal, and

(d) the consequences of non-compliance.

(5) Provision pursuant to sub-paragraph (1)(e) must secure that the grounds on which a person may appeal against a decision of the administrator include the following—

(a) that the decision was based on an error of fact;

(b) that the decision was wrong in law;

(c) in the case of a variable monetary penalty, that the amount of the penalty is unreasonable;

(d) in the case of a non-monetary discretionary requirement, that the nature of the requirement is unreasonable;

(e) that the decision was unreasonable for any other reason.

Discretionary requirements: enforcement+N.I.

14. (1)Provision under paragraph 12 may include provision for a person to pay a monetary penalty (a "non-compliance penalty") to an administrator if the person fails to comply with a non-monetary discretionary requirement imposed on the person.+N.I.

(2) Provision under sub-paragraph (1) may—

(a) specify the amount of the non-compliance penalty or provide for that amount to be determined in accordance with the regulations, or

(b) provide for the amount to be determined by the administrator or in some other way.

(3) If the regulations make provision within sub-paragraph (2)(b), they must, in relation to each

kind of failure for which a non-compliance penalty may be imposed—

(a) specify the maximum penalty that may be imposed for a failure of that kind, or

(b) provide for that maximum to be determined in accordance with the regulations.

(4) Provision under sub-paragraph (1) must secure that—

(a) the non-compliance penalty is imposed by notice served by the administrator, and

(b) the person on whom it is imposed may appeal against that notice.

(5) Provision pursuant to paragraph (b) of sub-paragraph (4) must secure that the grounds on which a person may appeal against a notice referred to in that sub-paragraph include the following—

(a) that the decision to serve the notice was based on an error of fact;

(b) that the decision was wrong in law;

(c) that the decision was unfair or unreasonable for any reason (including, in a case where the amount of the non-compliance penalty was determined by the administrator, that the amount is unreasonable).

Combination of sanctions+N.I.

15. (1)Provision may not be made under paragraphs 10 and 12 conferring powers on an administrator in relation to the same kind of breach of regulations under this Schedule unless it complies with the following requirements.+N.I.

(2) The provision must secure that the administrator may not serve a notice of intent referred to in paragraph 11. (1)(a) on a person in relation to a breach where a discretionary requirement has been imposed on that person in relation to the same breach.

(3) Such provision must secure that the administrator may not serve a notice of intent referred to in paragraph 13. (1)(a) on a person in relation to a breach where—

(a) a fixed monetary penalty has been imposed on that person in relation to the same breach, or

(b) the person has discharged liability to a fixed monetary penalty in relation to that breach pursuant to paragraph 11. (1)(b).

Monetary penalties+N.I.

16. (1)If the regulations confer power on an administrator to require a person to pay a fixed monetary penalty, a variable monetary penalty or a non-compliance penalty under paragraph 14. (1), they may include provision—+N.I.

(a) for early payment discounts;

(b) for the payment of interest or other financial penalties for late payment of the penalty, such interest or other financial penalties not in total to exceed the amount of that penalty;

(c) for enforcement of the penalty.

(2) Provision under sub-paragraph (1)(c) may include—

(a) provision for the administrator to recover the penalty, and any interest or other financial penalty for late payment, as a civil debt;

(b) provision for the penalty, and any interest or other financial penalty for late payment to be recoverable, on the order of a court, as if payable under a court order.

Costs recovery+N.I.

17. (1)Provision under paragraph 12 may include provision for an administrator, by notice, to require a person on whom a discretionary requirement is imposed to pay the costs incurred by the administrator in relation to the imposition of the discretionary requirement up to the time of its imposition.+N.I.

(2) In sub-paragraph (1), the reference to costs includes in particular—

(a) investigation costs;

(b) administration costs;

(c) costs of obtaining expert advice (including legal advice).

(3) Provision under this paragraph must secure that, in any case where a notice requiring payment of costs is served—

(a) the notice specifies the amount required to be paid;

(b) the administrator may be required to provide a detailed breakdown of that amount;

(c) the person required to pay costs is not liable to pay any costs shown by the person to have been unnecessarily incurred;

(d) the person required to pay costs may appeal against—

(i) the decision of the administrator to impose the requirement to pay costs;

(ii) the decision of the administrator as to the amount of those costs.

(4) Provision under this paragraph may include the provision referred to in paragraph 16. (1)(b) and (c) and (2).

(5) Provision under this paragraph must secure that the administrator is required to publish guidance about how the administrator will exercise the power conferred by the provision.

Appeals+N.I.

18. (1)The regulations may not provide for the making of an appeal other than to—+N.I.

(a) the First-tier Tribunal, or

(b) another tribunal created under an enactment.

(2) In sub-paragraph (1)(b) "tribunal" does not include an ordinary court of law.

(3) If the regulations make provision for an appeal in relation to the imposition of any requirement or service of any notice, they may include—

(a) provision suspending the requirement or notice pending determination of the appeal;

(b) provision as to the powers of the tribunal to which the appeal is made;

(c) provision as to how any sum payable in pursuance of a decision of that tribunal is to be recoverable.

(4) The provision referred to in sub-paragraph (3)(b) includes provision conferring on the tribunal to which the appeal is made power—

(a) to withdraw the requirement or notice;

(b) to confirm the requirement or notice;

(c) to take such steps as the administrator could take in relation to the act or omission giving rise to the requirement or notice;

(d) to remit the decision whether to confirm the requirement or notice, or any matter relating to that decision, to the administrator;

(e) to award costs.

Publicity for imposition of civil sanctions+N.I.

19. (1)The regulations may make provision enabling an administrator to give a publicity notice to a person on whom a civil sanction has been imposed in accordance with regulations under this Schedule.+N.I.

(2) A "publicity notice" is a notice requiring the person to publicise—

(a) the fact that the civil sanction has been imposed, and

(b) such other information as may be specified in the regulations,

in such manner as may be specified in the notice.

(3) The regulations may provide for a publicity notice to—

(a) specify the time for compliance with the notice, and

(b) require the person to whom it is given to supply an administrator with evidence of compliance within such time as may be specified in the notice.

(4) The regulations may provide that, if a person fails to comply with a publicity notice, an administrator may—
(a) publicise the information required to be publicised by the notice, and
(b) recover the costs of doing so from that person.

Persons liable to civil sanctions+N.I.

20. The regulations may make provision about the persons liable to civil sanctions under regulations under this Schedule and may (in particular) provide for—+N.I.
(a) the officers of a body corporate to be so liable as well the body corporate itself, and
(b) for the partners of a partnership to be liable as well as the partnership itself,
in such circumstances as may be specified.

Guidance as to use of civil sanctions+N.I.

21. (1)Where power is conferred on an administrator by the regulations to impose a civil sanction in relation to a breach of regulations under this Schedule, the provision conferring the power must secure that—+N.I.
(a) the administrator must publish guidance about the administrator's use of the civil sanction,
(b) the guidance must contain the relevant information,
(c) the administrator must revise the guidance where appropriate,
(d) the administrator must consult such persons as the provision may specify before publishing any guidance or revised guidance, and
(e) the administrator must have regard to the guidance or revised guidance in exercising the administrator's functions.
(2) In the case of guidance relating to a fixed monetary penalty, the relevant information referred to in sub-paragraph (1)(b) is information as to—
(a) the circumstances in which the penalty is likely to be imposed,
(b) the circumstances in which it may not be imposed,
(c) the amount of the penalty,
(d) how liability for the penalty may be discharged and the effect of discharge, and
(e) rights to make representations and objections and rights of appeal.
(3) In the case of guidance relating to a discretionary requirement, the relevant information referred to in sub-paragraph (1)(b) is information as to—
(a) the circumstances in which the requirement is likely to be imposed,
(b) the circumstances in which it may not be imposed,
(c) in the case of a variable monetary penalty, the matters likely to be taken into account by the administrator in determining the amount of the penalty (including, where relevant, any discounts for voluntary reporting of non-compliance), and
(d) rights to make representations and objections and rights of appeal.

Publication of enforcement action+N.I.

22. (1)Where power is conferred on an administrator by the regulations to impose a civil sanction in relation to a breach of regulations under this Schedule, the provision conferring the power must, subject to this paragraph, secure that the administrator must from time to time publish reports specifying—+N.I.
(a) the cases in which the civil sanction has been imposed, and
(b) where the civil sanction is a fixed monetary penalty, the cases in which liability to the penalty has been discharged pursuant to paragraph 11. (1)(b).
(2) In sub-paragraph (1)(a), the reference to cases in which the civil sanction has been imposed do

not include cases where the sanction has been imposed but overturned on appeal.

(3) The provision conferring the power need not secure the result in sub-paragraph (1) in cases where the relevant authority considers that it would be inappropriate to do so.

Compliance with regulatory principles+N.I.

23. A relevant national authority may not make any provision conferring power on an administrator to impose a civil sanction in relation to a breach of regulations under this Schedule unless the authority is satisfied that the administrator will act in accordance with the principles that—+N.I.

(a) regulatory activities should be carried out in a way that is transparent, accountable, proportionate and consistent;

(b) regulatory activities should be targeted only at cases in which action is needed.

Review+N.I.

24. (1)A relevant national authority must in accordance with this paragraph review the operation of any provision made by the authority conferring power on an administrator to impose a civil sanction in relation to a breach of regulations under this Schedule.+N.I.

(2) The review must take place as soon as practicable after the end of the period of three years beginning with the day on which the provision comes into force.

(3) The review must in particular consider whether the provision has implemented its objectives efficiently and effectively.

(4) In conducting a review under this paragraph the relevant national authority must consult such persons as the authority considers appropriate.

(5) The relevant national authority must publish the results of a review under this [F20section][F20paragraph].

[F21. (6)The relevant national authority must lay a copy of a review under this paragraph before—

(a) Parliament (where the relevant national authority is the Secretary of State);

(b) the National Assembly for Wales (where the relevant national authority is the Welsh Ministers);

(c) the Northern Ireland Assembly (where the relevant national authority is the Department of the Environment in Northern Ireland)].

Amendments (Textual)

F20. Word in Sch. 6 para. 24. (5) substituted (N.I.) (28.4.2014) by Carrier Bags Act (Northern Ireland) 2014 (c. 7), s. 8. (2)(a)

F21. Sch. 6 para. 24. (6) omitted (N.I.) (28.4.2014) by virtue of Carrier Bags Act (Northern Ireland) 2014 (c. 7), s. 8. (2)(b)

Suspension+N.I.

25. (1)Where provision has been made by a relevant national authority conferring power on an administrator to impose a civil sanction in relation to a breach of regulations under this Schedule, the authority may direct the administrator—+N.I.

(a) where the power is power to impose a fixed monetary penalty, not to serve any further notice of intent referred to in paragraph 11. (1)(a) in relation to a breach of that kind, and

(b) where the power is power to impose a discretionary requirement, not to serve any further notice of intent referred to in paragraph 13. (1)(a) in relation to a breach of that kind.

(2) The relevant national authority may only give a direction under sub-paragraph (1) in relation to a breach of regulations under this Schedule if it is satisfied that the administrator has failed on more than one occasion—

(a) to comply with any duty imposed on it under or by virtue of this Schedule in relation to a breach of that kind,

(b) to act in accordance with the guidance it has published in relation to a breach of that kind (in particular, the guidance published under paragraph 21), or

(c) to act in accordance with the principles referred to in paragraph 23 or with other principles of best practice in relation to the enforcement of a breach of that kind.

(3) The relevant national authority may by direction revoke a direction given by it under sub-paragraph (1) if satisfied that the administrator has taken the appropriate steps to remedy the failure to which that direction related.

(4) Before giving a direction under sub-paragraph (1) or (3) the relevant national authority must consult—

(a) the administrator, and

(b) such other persons as the authority considers appropriate.

(5) Where the relevant national authority gives a direction under this section, the authority must lay a copy before—

(a) Parliament (where the relevant national authority is the Secretary of State);

(b) the National Assembly for Wales (where the relevant national authority is the Welsh Ministers);

(c) the Northern Ireland Assembly (where the relevant national authority is the Department of the Environment in Northern Ireland).

(6) Where the relevant national authority gives a direction under this[F22 section][F22paragraph], the administrator must—

(a) publish the direction in such manner as the authority thinks fit, and

(b) take such other steps as the administrator thinks fit or the authority may require to bring the direction to the attention of other persons likely to be affected by it.

Amendments (Textual)

F22. Word in Sch. 6 para. 25. (6) substituted (N.I.) (28.4.2014) by Carrier Bags Act (Northern Ireland) 2014 (c. 7), s. 8. (3)

Payment of penalties into Consolidated Fund+N.I.

26. (1)Where pursuant to any provision made under this Schedule an administrator receives—+N.I.

(a) a fixed monetary penalty, a variable monetary penalty or a non-compliance penalty under paragraph 14,

(b) any interest or other financial penalty for late payment of such a penalty, or

(c) a sum paid in discharge of liability to a fixed monetary penalty pursuant to paragraph 11. (1)(b),

the administrator must pay it into the relevant Fund.

(2) In sub-paragraph (1) "relevant Fund" means—

(a) in a case where the administrator has functions only in relation to Wales, the Welsh Consolidated Fund,

(b) in a case where the administrator has functions only in relation to Northern Ireland, the Northern Ireland Consolidated Fund, and

(c) in any other case, the Consolidated Fund.

Part 3. +N.I.Procedures applying to regulations

Regulations made by a single authority+N.I.

27. (1)This paragraph applies in relation to an instrument containing regulations under this Schedule made by a single national authority.+N.I.

(2) Where the instrument contains regulations that—

(a) are to be made by the Secretary of State, and

(b) are subject to affirmative resolution procedure,

the regulations must not be made unless a draft of the statutory instrument containing them has been laid before and approved by a resolution of each House of Parliament.

(3) Where the instrument contains regulations that—

(a) are to be made by a national authority other than the Secretary of State, and

(b) are subject to affirmative resolution procedure,

the regulations must not be made unless a draft of the statutory instrument containing them has been laid before and approved by a resolution of the relevant devolved legislature.

(4) An instrument containing regulations made by the Secretary of State that are subject to negative resolution procedure is subject to annulment in pursuance of a resolution of either House of Parliament.

(5) An instrument containing regulations made by the Welsh Ministers that are subject to negative resolution procedure is subject to annulment in pursuance of a resolution of the National Assembly for Wales.

(6) An instrument containing regulations made by the Department of the Environment in Northern Ireland that are subject to negative resolution procedure is subject to negative resolution within the meaning of section 41. (6) of the Interpretation Act (Northern Ireland) 1954 (c. 33 (N.I.)) as if it were a statutory instrument within the meaning of that Act.

(7) Any provision that may be made by regulations subject to negative resolution procedure may be made by regulations subject to affirmative resolution procedure.

Regulations made by two or more national authorities+N.I.

28. (1)This paragraph applies in relation to an instrument containing regulations under this Schedule made or to be made by any two or more of—+N.I.

(a) the Secretary of State,

(b) the Welsh Ministers, and

(c) the Department of the Environment in Northern Ireland.

(2) If any of the regulations are subject to affirmative resolution procedure, all of them are subject to that procedure.

(3) Sub-paragraphs (2) to (6) of paragraph 27 apply to the instrument as they apply to an instrument containing regulations made by a single national authority.

(4) If in accordance with that paragraph—

(a) either House of Parliament resolves that an address be presented to Her Majesty praying that an instrument containing regulations made by the Secretary of State be annulled, or

(b) a devolved legislature resolves that an instrument containing regulations made by a national authority be annulled,

nothing further is to be done under the instrument after the date of the resolution and Her Majesty may by Order in Council revoke the instrument.

(5) This is without prejudice to the validity of anything previously done under the instrument or to the making of a new instrument.

(6) This paragraph applies in place of provision made by any other enactment about the effect of such a resolution.

Hybrid instruments+N.I.

29. If a draft of an instrument containing regulations under this Schedule would, apart from this paragraph, be treated for the purposes of the standing orders of either House of Parliament as a

hybrid instrument, it is to proceed in that House as if it were not such an instrument.+N.I.

Schedule 7. Renewable transport fuel obligations

Section 78

Introductory

1. Chapter 5 of Part 2 of the Energy Act 2004 (c. 20) (renewable transport fuel obligations) is amended as follows.

The Administrator

2. For section 125 (the Administrator) substitute—

"125. Appointment of the Administrator

(1) For the purposes of provision made by or under this Chapter, an RTF order may—
    (a) establish a body corporate, and
    (b) appoint that body as the Administrator.
(2) An RTF order may—
    (a) make provision for the appointment of members of the body;
    (b) make provision in relation to the staffing of the body;
    (c) make provision in relation to the expenditure of the body;
    (d) make provision regulating the procedure of the body;
    (e) make any other provision that the Secretary of State considers appropriate for purposes connected with the establishment and maintenance of the body.
(3) The provision that may be made by an RTF order by virtue of this section includes, in particular, provision conferring discretions on—
    (a) the Secretary of State;
    (b) the body itself; or
    (c) members or staff of the body.

125. AGeneral functions of the Administrator

(1) An RTF order may—
    (a) confer or impose powers and duties on the Administrator for purposes connected with the implementation of provision made by or under this Chapter;
    (b) confer discretions on the Administrator in relation to the making of determinations under such an order and otherwise in relation to the Administrator's powers and duties; and
    (c) impose duties on transport fuel suppliers for purposes connected with the Administrator's powers and duties (including, in particular, duties framed by reference to determinations made by the Administrator).
(2) It is the duty of the Administrator to promote the supply of renewable transport fuel whose production, supply or use—
    (a) causes or contributes to the reduction of carbon emissions, and
    (b) contributes to sustainable development or the protection or enhancement of the environment generally.

125. BFunctions of the Administrator: supplementary

(1) The powers that may be conferred on the Administrator by virtue of section 125. A(1) include, in particular—

(a) power to require a transport fuel supplier to provide the Administrator with such information as the Administrator may require for purposes connected with the carrying out of the Administrator's functions;

(b) power to impose requirements as to the form in which such information must be provided and as to the period within which it must be provided;

(c) power to imposes charges of specified amounts on transport fuel suppliers.

(2) The Secretary of State may give written directions to the Administrator about the exercise of any power conferred on the Administrator by virtue of subsection (1)(a) or (b).

(3) The power to give directions under subsection (2) includes power to vary or revoke the directions.

(4) The Administrator must comply with any directions given under that subsection.

(5) Sums received by the Administrator by virtue of provision within subsection (1)(c)—

(a) where the Administrator is the Secretary of State, must be paid into the Consolidated Fund, and

(b) otherwise, must be used for the purpose of meeting costs incurred in carrying out the Administrator's functions.

(6) The Secretary of State may make grants to the Administrator on such terms as the Secretary of State may determine.

125. CTransfer of functions to new Administrator

(1) The Secretary of State may by order—

(a) appoint a person as the Administrator ("the new Administrator") in place of a person previously so appointed by order under this Chapter ("the old Administrator"), and

(b) provide for the transfer of the functions of the old Administrator to the new Administrator.

(2) Only the following persons may be appointed as the Administrator by order under this section—

(a) the Secretary of State;

(b) a body or other person established or appointed by or under any enactment to carry out other functions;

(c) a body corporate established by the order for appointment as the Administrator.

(3) An order under this section that establishes a body for appointment as the Administrator may make any provision that may be made by an RTF order by virtue of section 125.

(4) An order under this section may provide for the transfer of staff of the old Administrator, and of any property, rights or liabilities to which the old Administrator is entitled or subject, to the new Administrator and may, in particular—

(a) provide for the transfer of any property, rights or liabilities to have effect subject to exceptions or reservations specified in or determined under the order;

(b) provide for the creation of interests in, or rights over, property transferred or retained or for the creation of new rights and liabilities;

(c) provide for the order to have effect in spite of anything that would prevent or restrict the transfer of the property, rights or liabilities otherwise than by the order.

(5) The order may, in particular—

(a) provide for anything done by or in relation to the old Administrator to have effect as if done by or in relation to the new Administrator;

(b) permit anything (which may include legal proceedings) which is in the process of being done by or in relation to the old Administrator when the transfer takes effect to be continued by or in relation to the new Administrator;

(c) provide for a reference to the old Administrator in an instrument or other document to be treated as a reference to the new Administrator;

(d) where the old Administrator was established by order under this Chapter, make provision for the dissolution of the old Administrator;

(e) make such modifications of any enactment relating to the old Administrator or the new Administrator as the Secretary of State considers appropriate for the purpose of facilitating the transfer.

(6) An order under this section that provides for the transfer of staff of the old Administrator to the new Administrator must make provision for the Transfer of Undertakings (Protection of Employment) Regulations 2006 to apply to the transfer.

(7) Subject to subsection (8), an order under this section is subject to the negative resolution procedure.

(8) The power to make an order under this section is subject to the affirmative resolution procedure if the order—

(a) contains provision by virtue of subsection (2)(c), or

(b) makes any modification of an enactment contained in—

(i) an Act of Parliament,

(ii) an Act of the Scottish Parliament,

(iii) a Measure or Act of the National Assembly for Wales, or

(iv) Northern Ireland legislation.".

Determination of amounts of transport fuel

3. In section 126 (determination of amounts of transport fuel), after subsection (4) insert—
"(5)If an RTF order makes provision for the counting or determination of amounts of transport fuel for the purposes of provision made by or under this Chapter by reference to any document, it may provide for references to the document to have effect as references to it as revised or re-issued from time to time.

(6) The Secretary of State may give written directions to the Administrator about the exercise of any of the Administrator's functions in connection with the counting or determination of amounts of transport fuel for the purposes of provision made by or under this Chapter.

(7) The power to give directions under subsection (6) includes power to vary or revoke the directions.

(8) The Administrator must comply with any directions given under that subsection.".

Discharge of obligation by payment

4. In section 128 (discharge of obligation by payment), for subsections (6) and (7) substitute—
"(6)Where the Administrator is the Secretary of State—

(a) sums received by the Administrator by virtue of this section must be paid into the Consolidated Fund, and

(b) an RTF order may make provision for sums to be paid by the Administrator to transport fuel suppliers, or to transport fuel suppliers of a specified description, in accordance with the specified system of allocation.

(7) Such an order must contain provision ensuring that the total of the sums so paid by the Administrator does not at any time exceed the total of the sums so received by the Administrator up to that time.

(8) Where the Administrator is a person other than the Secretary of State, an RTF order may—

(a) require the Administrator to use, to the specified extent, sums received by the Administrator by virtue of this section for the purpose of meeting costs incurred in carrying out the Administrator's functions, or

(b) require the Administrator to pay, to the specified extent, sums so received to the Secretary of

State.

(9) Sums so received which are not dealt with in accordance with provision made under subsection (8) must be paid by the Administrator to transport fuel suppliers, or to transport fuel suppliers of a specified description, in accordance with the specified system of allocation.

(10) The Secretary of State must pay sums received by the Secretary of State by virtue of provision made under subsection (8)(b) into the Consolidated Fund.".

Civil penalties

5. In section 129 (imposition of civil penalties), for subsection (7) substitute—

"(7)Sums received by the Administrator by virtue of this section—

    (a) where the Administrator is the Secretary of State, must be paid into the Consolidated Fund, and

    (b) otherwise, must be paid to the Secretary of State, who must pay them into the Consolidated Fund.".

Disclosure of information

6. After section 131 insert—

"131. ADisclosure of information held by Revenue and Customs

(1) This section applies to information held by or on behalf of the Commissioners for Her Majesty's Revenue and Customs in connection with their functions under or by virtue of the Hydrocarbon Oil Duties Act 1979.

(2) Such information may be disclosed to—

    (a) the Administrator, or

    (b) an authorised person,

for the purposes of or in connection with the Administrator's functions.

(3) In this Chapter "authorised person" means a person who—

    (a) provides services to, or exercises functions on behalf of, the Administrator, and

    (b) is authorised by the Administrator to receive information to which this section applies.

(4) The Administrator may authorise such a person to receive information to which this section applies either generally or for a specific purpose.

131. BFurther disclosure of information

(1) This section applies to information disclosed under section 131. A, other than information which is also provided to the Administrator or an authorised person otherwise than under that section.

(2) Information to which this section applies may not be disclosed—

    (a) by the Administrator,

    (b) by an authorised person, or

    (c) by any other person who obtains it in the course of providing services to, or exercising functions on behalf of, the Administrator,

except as permitted by the following provisions of this section.

(3) Subsection (2) does not apply to a disclosure made—

    (a) by the Administrator to an authorised person,

    (b) by an authorised person to the Administrator, or

    (c) by an authorised person to another authorised person,

for the purposes of, or in connection with, the discharge of the Administrator's functions.

(4) Subsection (2) does not apply to a disclosure if it is—

    (a) authorised by an enactment,

    (b) made in pursuance of an order of a court,

    (c) made for the purposes of a criminal investigation or criminal proceedings (whether or not within the United Kingdom) relating to a matter in respect of which the Administrator has functions,

    (d) made for the purposes of civil proceedings (whether or not within the United Kingdom) relating to a matter in respect of which the Administrator has functions,

    (e) made with the consent of the Commissioners for Her Majesty's Revenue and Customs, or

    (f) made with the consent of each person to whom the information relates.

131. CWrongful disclosure

(1) A person commits an offence if—

    (a) he discloses information about a person in contravention of section 131. B(2), and

    (b) the person's identity is specified in the disclosure or can be deduced from it.

(2) In subsection (1) "information about a person" means revenue and customs information relating to a person within the meaning of section 19. (2) of the Commissioners for Revenue and Customs Act 2005 (wrongful disclosure).

(3) It is a defence for a person charged with an offence under this section to prove that he reasonably believed—

    (a) that the disclosure was lawful, or

    (b) that the information had already and lawfully been made available to the public.

(4) A person guilty of an offence under this section is liable—

    (a) on conviction on indictment, to imprisonment for a term not exceeding two years or a fine or both, or

    (b) on summary conviction, to imprisonment for a term not exceeding twelve months or a fine not exceeding the statutory maximum or both.

(5) A prosecution for an offence under this section—

    (a) may be brought in England and Wales only with the consent of the Director of Public Prosecutions;

    (b) may be brought in Northern Ireland only with the consent of the Director of Public Prosecutions for Northern Ireland.

(6) In the application of this section—

    (a) in England and Wales, in relation to an offence committed before the commencement of section 154. (1) of the Criminal Justice Act 2003, or

    (b) in Northern Ireland,

the reference in subsection (4)(b) to twelve months is to be read as a reference to six months.".

Interpretation

7. (1)Section 132. (1) (interpretation of Chapter 5 of Part 2) is amended as follows.

(2) For the definition of "Administrator" substitute—

""Administrator" means the person for the time being appointed as the Administrator by order under this Chapter;".

(3) In the appropriate place insert—

""authorised person" has the meaning given by section 131. A(3);";

""enactment" includes—

(a) an enactment contained in subordinate legislation,

(b) an enactment contained in, or in an instrument made under, an Act of the Scottish Parliament,

(c) an enactment contained in, or in an instrument made under, Northern Ireland legislation, and

(d) an enactment contained in, or in an instrument made under, a Measure or Act of the National

Assembly for Wales;".

(4) In section 196. (1) of the Energy Act 2004 (c. 20) (general interpretation), in the definition of "enactment", after " "enactment"" insert " (except in Chapter 5 of Part 2) ".

Schedule 8. Carbon emissions reduction targets

Section 79

Gas Act 1986 (c. 44)

1. (1)Section 33. BC of the Gas Act 1986 (promotion of reductions in carbon emissions: gas transporters and gas suppliers) is amended as follows.
(2) After subsection (1) insert—
"(1. A)The power to make orders under this section may be exercised so as to impose more than one carbon emissions reduction obligation on a person in relation to the same period or to periods that overlap to any extent.".
(3) In subsection (5) (provision that may be made by an order under section 33. BC in relation to the obligations it imposes), after paragraph (b) insert—
   "(ba)requiring the whole or any part of a carbon emissions reductions target to be met by action relating to—
(i) persons of a specified description,
(ii) specified areas or areas of a specified description, or
(iii) persons of a specified description in specified areas or areas of a specified description;".
(4) In subsection (13) (interpretation), at the appropriate place insert—
""specified" means specified in the order.".

Electricity Act 1989 (c. 29)

2. In section 6. (9) of the Electricity Act 1989 (definition of "electricity distributor" and "electricity supplier"), at the appropriate place insert—
""electricity generator" means any person who is authorised by a generation licence to generate electricity except where that person is acting otherwise than for purposes connected with the carrying on of activities authorised by the licence;".
3. (1)Section 41. A of that Act (promotion of reductions in carbon emissions: electricity distributors and electricity suppliers) is amended as follows.
(2) In subsection (1) (power by order to impose obligations on distributors and suppliers to achieve carbon emissions reductions targets)—
(a) before paragraph (a) insert—
   "(za)on each electricity generator (or each electricity generator of a specified description);", and
(b) in the closing words, before "distributor" insert " generator, ".
(3) After that subsection insert—
"(1. A)The power to make orders under this section may be exercised so as to impose more than one carbon emissions reduction obligation on a person in relation to the same period or to periods that overlap to any extent.".
(4) In subsection (3) (power for order to specify criteria by reference to which the Gas and Electricity Markets Authority is to determine targets), before "electricity distributors" insert " electricity generators, ".
(5) In subsection (4) (duty of the Secretary of State and the Authority to carry out functions under the section in a way that does not inhibit competition), for the words from "no electricity distributor" to the end of the subsection substitute "—

(a) no electricity generator is unduly disadvantaged in competing with other electricity generators,

(b) no electricity distributor is unduly disadvantaged in competing with other electricity distributors, and

(c) no electricity supplier is unduly disadvantaged in competing with other electricity suppliers.".

(6) In subsection (5) (provision that may be made by an order in relation to the obligations it imposes)—

(a) in paragraph (a), before "electricity distributors" insert " electricity generators, ",

(b) after paragraph (b) insert—

"(ba)requiring the whole or any part of a carbon emissions reductions target to be met by action relating to—

(i) persons of a specified description,

(ii) specified areas or areas of a specified description, or

(iii) persons of a specified description in specified areas or areas of a specified description;",

(c) in paragraph (d), before "distributors" insert " generators, ", and

(d) in paragraph (f), before "distributors" insert " generators, ".

(7) In subsection (6) (power for order to authorise the Authority to require the provision of information), before "distributor" insert " generator, ".

(8) In subsection (7)(d) (power for order to make provision for transfer of person's target to another distributor or supplier or to a gas transporter or supplier), before "electricity distributor" insert " electricity generator, ".

(9) In subsection (8)(d) (power for order to make different provision in relation to different distributors or suppliers), before "distributors" insert " generators, ".

(10) In subsection (11) (duty to consult before making order), before "electricity distributors" insert " electricity generators, ".

(11) In subsection (13) (interpretation), at the appropriate place insert—

""specified" means specified in the order.".

(12) In the heading, before "electricity distributors" insert " electricity generators, ".

4. (1)Section 42. AA of that Act (publication of statistical information about performance of suppliers and distributors) is amended as follows.

(2) In subsection (1) (duty of Gas and Electricity Consumer Council to publish information about performance and consumer complaints)—

(a) in paragraph (a), before "electricity suppliers" insert " electricity generators, ", and

(b) in paragraph (b), before "suppliers" insert " generators, ".

(3) In subsection (2) (definition of "complaints"), before "electricity suppliers" insert " electricity generators, ".

5. In section 64. (1) of that Act (interpretation etc of Part 1), in the definition of "electricity distributor" and "electricity supplier", after " "electricity distributor"" insert " , "electricity generator" .

Utilities Act 2000 (c. 27)

6. (1)Section 103 of the Utilities Act 2000 (overall carbon emissions reduction targets) is amended as follows.

(2) In subsection (1)(b) (power by order to specify overall target for the promotion of measures mentioned in section 41. A(2) of the 1989 Act), before "distributors" insert " generators, ".

(3) After subsection (1) insert—

"(1. A)The power conferred by this section may be exercised so as to specify more than one overall target in relation to the same period or to periods that overlap to any extent.".

(4) In subsection (2)(b) (power for order to specify criteria for apportionment of overall target between electricity and gas sectors), before "electricity distributors" insert " electricity generators,

".
(5) In subsection (4) (duty to consult before making order), before "electricity distributors" insert " electricity generators, ".

Open Government Licence v3.0

Contains public sector information licensed under the Open Government Licence v3.0.
The full licence if available at the following address:
http://www.nationalarchives.gov.uk/doc/open-government-licence/version/3/

Printed in Great Britain
by Amazon

82094146R00052